DATE DUE

3 1 MAY 1972   PAT

THEOLOGY OF EXISTENCE

Theology of Existence

by

Fritz Buri

Translated by
Harold H. Oliver and Gerhard Onder

THE ATTIC PRESS
Greenwood, S. C.
1965

TRANSLATOR'S PREFACE

To many American theologians and theological students the name of Fritz Buri is associated with an extreme "left wing" attack on Rudolf Bultmann summed up in Buri's own word: "de-kerygmatizing" (*Entkerygmatisierung*).[1] Many recent theological works[2] appraise him only in terms of his earlier position and hence fail to take into account his transformation from the Neo-Schweitzerian School of "Consistent Eschatology" to an independent existential theology proposed first in this volume only now being offered in English. While Buri would probably be embarrassed if we should speak of "the later Buri," it is nevertheless true that his present theological position lacks the antidogmatic emphasis of his Bernese mentor, the late Martin Werner.

It may seem to some that Buri, a long-time critic of Neo-

[1] This position was presented in the essay: "Entmythologisierung oder Entkerygmatisierung der Theologie," *Kerygma und Mythos*: Diskussion und Stimmen des In- und Auslandes (Theologische Forschung 2), 1952, pp. 85-101.

[2] Two American works have given considerable attention to Buri: John Macquarrie, *The Scope of Demythologizing: Bultmann and his Critics* (New York: Harper & Brothers, 1960), pp. 130-53, and Schubert Ogden, *Christ Without Myth* (New York: Harper & Brothers, 1961), pp. 105-111. Of the two, only Ogden seems to be conscious that *Theologie der Existenz* represents a significant 'turn' in Buri's thinking.

Orthodoxy, has become more sympathetic with this conservative European movement at a time when others have moved on to other things. For example, the post-Bultmannians such as Fuchs and Ebeling (with Ott) have made explorations in the direction of the later Heidegger; certain Americans have turned to such emphases as Whiteheadian philosophy (Ogden and Cobb) and a new "secular" theology (Altizer, van Buren and Hamilton). Before Buri is written off for his return to a more sympathetic appraisal of the Christian tradition, we would do well to examine this programmatic essay in which Jaspersian philosophy has become the basis for a liberal theology which may well speak to modern man in a "world come of age."

Buri, Hauptpfarrer of the Basel Münster and Ausserordentlicher Professor in the University of Basel, has consistently sought to relate the Christian message to the rapidly changing situation in the modern world. During the heyday of Neo-Orthodoxy he stood up against its presuppositional supernaturalism and theological literalism;[3] in the mid-thirties he spoke out strongly against the dangers of German *Seinsreligion*;[4] and, since the Second World War he has engaged in a vigorous criticism of the dangerous elements inherent in the Heideggerian *Seinsfrage*, though conscious of some of its creative possibilities for a Christian theology.[5] In recent years he has devoted much of his time to the completion of a multi-volume dogmatics, entitled: *Dogmatik als Selbstverständnis des christlichen Glaubens* (Vol. I, 1956; Vol. II, 1962). In this work, still untranslated, one finds the mature theological reflections

[3] For example, "Um den Offenbarungsglauben," *Schweizerische theologische Umschau*, 5 (1935, March), 201-10.

[4] "Sein, Sinn und Eschaton: Zur Auseinandersetzung zwischen Christentum und deutscher Glaubensbewegung," *Schweizerische theologische Umschau*, 5 (1935, March), 245-58 and 6 (1936), 13-15.

[5] "Theologie zwischen—oder mit Jaspers und Heidegger," *Schweizerische theologische Umschau*, 30 (1960, July), 83-94.

of a gifted philosophical mind which is oriented to a positive appraisal and interpretation of theology past and present.

As all translations, this one too is a "labor of love." The personal affection between the two translators, and the sincere appreciation which I have for Professor Buri are here interwoven in a tangible product representing our common effort. The translators hope that through their labors the live option which Buri's theology affords will receive serious consideration in the English-speaking world.

The translators are especially grateful to Prof. Buri for kindly agreeing to review the translation in rough draft, to Dr. John E. Steely of Wake Forest for his invaluable suggestions at many critical points, and to the alumni of The Southeastern Baptist Theological Seminary whose special fund for faculty projects aided in the secretarial expenses of this volume.

HAROLD H. OLIVER

Wake Forest, North Carolina
April 8, 1965

FOREWORD TO THE
ENGLISH EDITION

It is neither the custom nor desire of everyone to read thick books in order to clarify his own religious questions and theological problems, or even to orient himself to a theologian and his views. For this reason the present little volume may be able to render a good service to those of our time who are interested in religion. It offers not only an easily mastered introduction to my theological thought-world, which I have since undertaken to unfold more comprehensively in my *Dogmatik als Selbstverständnis des christlichen Glaubens* ("Dogmatics as Self-Understanding of the Christian Faith"), of which two volumes have already appeared; it contains as well the program for this dogmatic system and therefore touches upon the most important points with which Christian faith always deals when it attempts, with respect to its tradition and in view of the current spiritual situation, to become clear about its basic stance and essential contents. In this programmatic essay the reader finds therefore a *Glaubenslehre in nuce*— or better said, *in statu nascendi*, that is, in its formative stage, in its first draft.

Living thinking about faith is always provisional. It originates from a more or less precisely fixed or even shattered formulation of faith which it questions, and then drafts a new conception and formulation of what has been transmitted to it which is to be valid for today and tomorrow. In this constant involvement of living theological thought in the stream of history, in which the past always newly becomes present and new movements and horizons appear, there are for the individual thinker or entire generations turning points in which the transitions and transformations stand out in a special way. It lies in the nature of the thing that such situations—like the waters upon which one travels—are characterized by all sorts of whirlpools and disturbances, or from the perspective of the traveler—by powerful impacts and devastating upheavals. For our current theological and ecclesiastical position such a situation has resulted from the appearance of so-called "Neo-Orthodoxy," which—despite orthodox terminology— is more avantgardistic than the theological liberalism out of which it arose, but which because of this heritage is anything but orthodox.

The *Theology of Existence* shares in this transitional situation which is typical for the Protestant theology and Church. In my own theological development this document represents the arrival of a new phase. Formerly I proceeded from the "thorough-going" eschatological conception of Christianity represented by Albert Schweitzer, from the insights which derive from this for the understanding of the "history of dogma" development of Christianity, and from the attempt, over against the "case history" approach to Christianity, to validate the truth of the primitive Christian expectation of the Kingdom of God and Pauline "Christ-mysticism" in a cultural ethic determined by the principle of "Reverence for Life." From this view of the New Testament, of Christian dogmatic development and its corresponding deformation—a view inspired by Albert

Schweitzer and my former teacher, Martin Werner—was produced my book *Christlicher Glaube in dieser Zeit* (1952) which (an irony of the history of theology!) will appear simultaneously with the *Theology of Existence* in an English translation published by Macmillan.

Although between the original publication dates of the two writings lay only a span of two years, they are in attitude and content quite different. I had certainly been occupied quite early with Heidegger and Jaspers, but had heard them only in a special way or had rejected them, essentially from the perspective of the intellectual-theoretical positivism of the Vienna school—above all, of Moritz Schlick—under whose influence I then stood. After the preparation of the lectures which only some time later came out under the title, *Christlicher Glaube in dieser Zeit,* Karl Jaspers' philosophy became for me so powerful, that I began to understand not only the impossibility of Heideggerian existentialism—and since, also his non-objectifying thinking about Being—, but also the inadequacy of the rationalism of the Vienna school and of "thorough-going" eschatology. I should not like to deny that—even amidst simultaneous, violent resistance—I have learned something from Neo-Orthodoxy and gained a new rapport with the content of the Christian tradition.

Thus I came likewise to an about-face, which was first decisively expressed in the "Theology of Existence" and has been occasionally compared by critics with the difference between Schleiermacher's *Reden* and his *Glaubenslehre.* Not to speak of the otherwise inappropriateness of this comparison, it is somewhat strained, because, to begin with, to contrast with the products of my somewhat wild theological youth, which was occupied along with ordinary theology above all with the world-views of poets, I had not a dogmatics, but only the draft of one.

From the egg of the *Theology of Existence,* which I once laid with a few cackles, two considerable volumes of dogmatics have since emerged, and a further is about to be hatched. If in the execution of the program proposed there these volumes do not renounce their emergence out of that breeding which examiners of theological pedigree may label as a cross between existential philosophy and Neo-Orthodoxy, nevertheless many a thing has appeared otherwise than was originally planned, and I would not now be in a position simply to subscribe to or repeat everything which I expressed in the *Theology of Existence.* Not only does the term "existence" scarcely appear in my *Dogmatik,* it has been replaced by the more pregnant and hermeneutically comprehensive concept of the "self-understanding of the Christian faith." More significant still, the whole structure of the dogmatics has changed from what was foreseen in the first draft. In the dogmatics, after the Prolegomena dealing with theoretical knowledge, I begin the positive execution of the system not with the doctrine of God, but rather with that of man and grace—from the insight that "God for Existence" can legitimately be spoken of in the Christian sense only on the basis of the saving work of Christ. In contradistinction to the original plan of the dogmatics, it has occurred to me in the meantime that the "Fulness of the Godhead" which is known in Christ can only be unfolded at the conclusion of the dogmatics, that is, not merely on the basis of soteriology, but only after this has been unfolded in the doctrines of creation and Providence, as well as in eschatology and ecclesiology.

Even if in these eschatological and ecclesiological parts of the dogmatics dedicated to the problem of history, perspectives of the "thorough-going" eschatology (that is, original principles of my theology) have been validated in other aspects, there lies nevertheless a great distance between this doctrine of God as the "Fulness of Being" in Christ and its biographical beginnings in Albert Schweitzer's view of the primitive Christian faith in the Kingdom of God. In the theology of existence indeed the "eggshells" of "thorough-going" eschatology are still visible. If I was there already no longer of the opinion—as was Martin Werner—that "thorough-going" eschatology was the single key for understanding Christian tradition, I nevertheless still spoke there quite uncritically of the messianic self-consciousness of the historical Jesus and undertook accordingly to construct a "Christology" out of its historical problematic.

Although I am conscious today of the dubiousness of this "Christology of Existence" and especially of the untenability of the Schweitzerian view of the primitive Christian proclamation, I have altered none of this for the English edition. This is not the place to replace that Christological attempt, which is in some instances a mistaken construction, with a doctrine of the person and work of Christ which I have in the meantime developed in my *Dogmatik*. The *Dogmatik* has been freed from those unsuitable elements and in it the factor of the delayed Parousia has been put in a new light by reckoning with the self-understanding of the faith, which is not a psychological-historical phenomenon. Such a correction would almost double the size of the present volume.

I take pleasure on this occasion in recalling numerous and fruitful conversations in which these questionable points afforded the translator of this writing and me the opportunity, as we strove together, to find the best formulation of these thoughts in a language which does not correspond exactly to the form in which they were originally thought through. Thus we were able once again to experience the fact that the English language is an excellent instrument for clarifying profundity—or even nonsense—thought up by the Germanic mind. Whether we succeeded to the simplicity required by English syntax we leave to the judgment of the reader of this translation. May he take it as it is intended: as an introduction to a world of faith which offers material and work to be thought through and developed for a whole life-time. Perhaps we shall meet sometime at a farther station on this theological course of thinking which was opened to me here and to which this translation will provide access now to the English-speaking public. Until then, on a course of theological thinking which dares to start with the existence of the believer, I greet the new traveling companions from across the ocean with the promising confession of the Apostle Paul:

When I was a child, I spoke like a child, I thought like a child, I reasoned like a child; when I became a man, I gave up childish ways. For now we see in a mirror dimly, but then face to face. Now I know in part, then I shall understand fully, even as I have been fully understood (I Cor. 13: 11f. RSV).

FRITZ BURI

January 30, 1965

CONTENTS

INTRODUCTION

The term "existence" is used in current theology and philosophy frequently and in various ways. Since we wish to develop here a theology of existence, it is necessary to say in advance what we mean by this term. At the same time we are provided an opportunity to show how we come to speak of a theology of existence, and to give an introductory survey of the whole of our purpose.

From the time of Kierkegaard on and in agreement with significant usage of present-day existential philosophy, the following factors are important to us for the nature of existence:

1. Existence indicates an authentic being (*Selbstsein*) which I am not able to prove scientifically, *i.e.* with universal validity, to myself or to others. This reality is disclosed to me only in a non-objectifiable self-awareness (*Innewerden meiner selbst*), through which alone I become what I am.

2. In this self-realization (*Selbstverwirklichung*), however, existence is not at all concerned merely with itself. It is experienced therein rather as related to Transcendence as the source of itself and of Being in general, which is not to be objectified, but only believed.

1

3. Existence becomes conscious of this relation to Transcendence as a "reception of itself as a gift" (*Sichgeschenktbekommen*) in the freedom of responsibility against the background of the possibility that it can fail to take place, that it can miss and lose its authentic being.

4. From such a self-understanding there is gained for existence a new access to the world of mythology, of philosophical speculation and of religious dogmas as forms of expression of the self-understanding of and for existence.

5. To existence belongs finally the confession of its historicality, *i.e.* the acceptance of the limitations of all its realizations in unlimited ways, valid only for it and therefore not to be generalized. In the community of self-existing beings made possible by it, the eternal realm of truth makes its temporal appearance.

Already from these statements, only intimated so far, but more precisely to be worked out and tested in what follows, it may have become evident that this term "existence" is *theologically* important. Upon each of the individually cited characteristics of being there obtrude directly the corresponding concepts of theological dogmatics.

The delimitation of the self-disclosure of existence in the non-objectifiable self-awareness (*Selbstvergewisserung*) over against the scientific way to knowledge allows us to think formally of the theological difference between knowledge and revelatory faith.

Not only formally, but also materially, the relation of existence to Transcendence as the origin of itself and of Being is in harmony with the doctrine of God and His relation to the world.

Likewise evident is the parallel between the theological doctrine of the Fall of man and grace, and the knowledge of existence as "ability to fall" (*Verfallenkönnen*) and "reception of itself as a gift" (*Sichgeschenktbekommen*).

On the significance of the understanding of myth which is given with this concept of existence nothing special needs to be said in view of the present discussion of the problem of demythologizing, especially in reference to Christology.

Also in regard to the last point, that is, the historicality of existence and its realization in community as the appearance in time of the realm of truth, there is present the correspondence of the realization of salvation in time and eternity to the theological representations.

We are now concerned however not merely with establishing these general references between the different aspects of our term "existence" and the individual doctrinal points of theological dogmatics. The real significance of the concept of existence first appears when we become conscious that these dogmatic *loci* furnish the traditional arrangement of Christian dogmatics, a dogmatics which in past and present is by no means a self-contained, unified whole. In reality, it is much more the case that concepts like revelation, God and His creation, sin and grace, the person and work of the Redeemer, Church and consummation indicate just those points at which the problematic character of theology has most clearly appeared, because here the most antithetical concepts are placed over against each other. Several references will illustrate this:

Theology appeals to revelation. But does it deal therein with a general revelation conceivable also by reason, or with a special revelation accessible only to faith? We know the controversy over natural theology, correct interpretation of Scripture and the scientific character of theology.

Theology makes pronouncements about God and His relationship to the world. Accordingly as it deals with natural and revealed theology it takes different positions toward the proofs for the existence of God, the question of the personality of God, the question of miracle and the problem of theodicy.

In the doctrine of salvation the different conceptions envisage self-redemption or redemption from without. Sin is rendered inoffensive or demonized; grace is made superfluous or available.

In Christology the different conceptions of the personality of the Redeemer and his work of salvation are placed in contrast: the God-man of dogma, the so-called historical Jesus and the eschatological Christ. Wherein lies the significance of this phenomenon so rich in manifold conceptions?

The opposites naturally work themselves out in soteriology and Christology, as well as in the doctrine of the means of salvation, the Church and Last Things. The demythologizing dissolution of *Heilsgeschichte* is bound up with the absolutizing of cultural forms, and *heilsgeschichtlich* constructions appear as magic and mythology. The different assertions about the salvation appearing in history through Christ compete with each other as truth.

This is the situation in which the concept of existence indicated for us at the outset now gains decisive significance. This concept stands not only in formal and material analogy to the conceptuality of Christian theology, but—as we just reminded ourselves—that which customarily appears in such a problematic form in this conceptuality can from the point of view of the concept of existence be validated in appropriate and tenable ways.

Revelation in general and in relation to Scripture can be spoken of correctly only when it is understood in connection with existence.

God for existence: that is the point of view from which the problems of the doctrine of God and the world, the questions of the provability of God, His personhood, miracle and evil in the world can be answered.

Sin and guilt, forgiveness and new creation become realities for existence which is understood as grace.

In a Christology of existence the problem of demythologizing is also solved in a positive way.

The means of salvation, Church, conceptions of the beyond and of the end-time maintain their significance as forms of the mediation, realization and expression of Christian existence in time.

On this basis and in this sense one should speak of the theology of existence. Precisely in the application of the formal and material points of view contained in the concept of existence our term "existence" will prove its capacity for truth and reality, as well as its tenability, in the discussion of the traditional theological conceptuality. Whether, in view of the present situation in theology and of the more detached attitude of existential philosophy over against theology, this understanding can still hold as a theology of existence and is not to be designated as philosophy of existence,—of that we shall have to speak in the first chapter, "Revelation and Existence," to which we now turn our attention after this introductory survey.

CHAPTER 1

REVELATION AND EXISTENCE

The Old Protestant dogmaticians customarily gave priority in their systems to the two doctrines of revelation and Holy Scripture. In the former they distinguished between a general, natural knowledge of God through reason and a supernatural revelation of God in the Scriptures, accessible only to faith. The rational knowledge of God was divided into an innate knowledge and a knowledge acquired on the basis of nature and history. As to the application of the term revelation in this sphere, it was cautiously reserved for the special revelation in Scripture and the salvation activity resulting from it. In this revelation, which alone sufficed for salvation, a further distinction was made between a direct revelation which became available to the authors of the Holy Scripture through inspiration, and an indirect which can occur in us through the Scripture used as a means of salvation under the testimony of the Holy Spirit. Over against Catholic theology which substituted for this the ecclesiastical teaching office as the norm of scriptural revelation, Old Protestant orthodoxy developed with special completeness the doctrine of Scripture, the theory of its inspiration, and the rules for its correct exegesis.

In place of both of these points of departure there appeared in the newer protestantism the so-called Prolegomena of dogmatics, in which the scientific character of the doctrine of faith (*Glaubenslehre*) was established epistemologically and in a religio-philosophical or psychological manner. That happened principally with the result either that out of the religious and Christian consciousness the Christian principle was derived as a universally valid truth which was then used as a normative arrangement of the Christian tradition, or that an attempt was made to justify scientifically a special religious experience of the historical figure of Jesus.

This Neo-Protestant ground of dogmatics is today rejected by a new "theology of revelation" as a false natural theology and a betrayal of revelation. However, since that which in due course led principally to this Neo-Protestantism is still in force, namely, modern man's understanding of himself, the world and history, freed from the shackles of dogma, this theology sees itself placed anew before the problem of natural theology, the question of the correct exegesis of Scripture and the question of the relation of theology, philosophy and science.

What can be said from the perspective of a theology of existence about these much-discussed problems of the relationship of general knowledge of God and revelatory faith, of hermeneutics and the scientific character of theology?

1.   REASON AND REVELATION

Viewed from the concept of existence, the cause of this controversy over the possibility of a rational knowledge of God seems to lie in the ambiguity of the term "reason." It is already in itself a contradiction, to be sure, when a theology of existence for the sake of revelation believes that it must contest the competence of reason in matters of the knowledge of God. For it can only do this with the aid of reason, turning with its arguments toward reasonable individuals, although in unreasonable ways. To be sure, it can thereby have in view a certain concept of reason which to a certain extent justifies this struggle against reason, for there is in natural theology a conception of reason which actually deals with revelation in a very limited way. Reason is here understood in the sense of a universally valid, scientific proof—just that kind of objective knowledge which, as we have said in reference to our concept of existence may not be able to conceive of the reality meant by it. From the perspective of existence it appears therefore as an impractical absolutizing when, in the name of so-called scientific thought, the faith of revelation is contested. Existence in any case knows itself related to its transcendent origin in ways which are objectively inconceivable. From the standpoint of existence, therefore, it must be considered an inversion to wish to establish or justify the faith of revelation scientifically. Actually that can only lead to a betrayal of revelation, and signifies also a misunderstanding of reason. Reason is more than mere rational conceptuality. It comprises also existence, and is therefore open to its relation to Transcendence. Nevertheless, before we pursue this line, we must first show how even objective, rational knowledge, when it stays within its boundaries, can know about revelation.

It is not only in relation to existence that conceptual knowledge experiences the boundaries of its competence; rather, already in the sphere of its objectifiable world it arrives at boundaries which it cannot cross unless it abandons itself. There are two aspects to its limited character.

First, there is for scientific knowledge no possibility of a total view of the world. Reality is not such that it can be conceived under only one point of view and by means of only one method of research. Categories which are highly fruitful in one sphere prove to be quite inappropriate in another, or—if used nevertheless—produce distortion and loss of comprehension. There is no universal method, no all-encompassing point of view. Every scientist knows that the more precisely and adequately he examines his object, the sharper and more suitable are the results. Final questions, like "Why is there something, and not nothing?", which deal with the whole of reality are scientifically completely worthless; it may be that they even demonstrate the potential boundary of scientific knowledge.

The limited character of science is demonstrated in yet another direction. Conceptual thinking never deals with the object in itself, but only with appearances. It is always our object world with which we deal. Being an object, however, means being related to a subject. Whether we turn this way or that—in conceptual knowledge we do not escape the subject-object split. We can probably change the points of view and rearrange the different aspects, but we must become one with the object itself in order to be able to grasp it in its entirety. That we can never achieve—with the exception of that which we designate as existence; universally valid scientific method stops right here.

To wish to grasp something where there is nothing more to be grasped means to be unreasonable. It belongs to the reason of knowledge also to perceive and acknowledge its own boundaries. Where *ratio* does that, namely, comprehends its finitude and accepts it, there it is led by reason. And there it perceives something which, if it does not press to its boundaries, or if it wishes to cross over them, it will never perceive, namely, the voice of the revelation of that which is not the world, namely, the reality of Transcendence.

The understanding, however, possesses no categories for

making a pronouncement about this reality; for with each such pronouncement it would overstep the boundaries set for it and thereby lose the place at which it alone is able to hear this voice. Because it is not the nature of conceptual knowledge to persist there in dumb devotion where there is nothing more to be perceived, it does not remain at the boundary, staring into the Naught, but turns itself again to its own world in which it is at home. It is, however, not now so self-evidently and absolutely "at home" as before its view into infinitude and with it the revelation of its own finitude.

In contrast to the situation in Old Protestant orthodoxy sketched in the beginning we should like to speak more decisively about a general revelation than was there the case—quite apart from the assertion of a knowledge of God on this basis. The concept of general revelation represented by us does not permit us in any case to make any pronouncements about God. It can neither draft an idea of God nor, on the basis of nature and history, become closed to a first Cause or Creator. For such speculations to be legitimate for reason, they must be able to ground themselves on something other than conceptual knowledge. Such speculations of reason which exceed the boundaries of objectivity are only possible where reason is grounded in existence. Existence certainly belongs also to reason, and thus reason knows also of another revelation than that of the Naught at the boundary of conceptual knowledge, namely, the revelation of God for existence in faith.

2.   REVELATION FOR EXISTENCE

We are dealing here primarily with the revelation of a boundary of conceptual-objective knowledge. Here, however, knowledge does not direct itself to the world, nor to its own structure, but to the knower himself. The subject of the act of knowledge, as well as the act of knowledge which he performs, belong to the objectifiable, scientific, universally valid, knowable world. This world is in none of its appearances and therefore also not in my knowledge the whole or the absolute, but is always something finite. Like the physical world, so also the psychical permits itself to be conceived in general categories and to be objectively known. Understanding in this mental and personal sphere demands not merely other categories than the explanation of things and events outside this realm. The different possibilities of explaining the psycho-spiritual indicate that conceptual knowledge here approaches a new boundary.

This boundary of objective knowledge in relation to the knower himself appears in a three-fold manner: First, in such a way that I can never ultimately observe myself. As Being-in-itself resists every objectivation, so I also, the subject of the subject-object relation, cannot make an object of myself. It is probably still possible to objectify this situation as a general certainty of knowledge—but just the situation of knowledge alone, and not that which is concrete in the situation, namely, the subject of the transcendental perspective. It is only a picture of this impossibility of self-objectification when we recall that the eye which sees, cannot see itself. That I am I; that I and not just anything else thinks in me—this secret of the unity of the person which in its actual enactment is something other than the demonstrable biographical connection, I can prove neither to another nor to myself. I can only enact this unity and illuminate it for myself in objectively "foundering" consciousness.

To this first consideration can be added a second: So far as I am able objectively to account for my situation, I know myself involved in unending connections in which I operate, but at the same time experience myself as dependent and limited. Something other than such an involvement in a boundless complex of activities and dependencies cannot be established with universal validity. Also, unless one's own possibilities of action are surveyed, he cannot yet speak of freedom. Responsibility can never be established with absolute certainty. Whoever does not wish to be responsible can always find an alibi.

However, with the acknowledgment of a general causal connection, which is not placed in question by the current concept of the so-called laws of nature as merely statistical regularity, a reality is now touched upon which belongs to the nature of my personality. Though determined and dependent, I know myself nevertheless to be responsible for my attitude and the actions which proceed from it. At every moment it is I who decide what I am. What I am depends upon what I decide. This action is also a necessity, but a necessity in which I experience myself at the same time as free. I would annihilate myself if I did not wish to admit this responsibility. I exist only in decision. This situation of existence cannot be proved. I can become aware of it only in objectively "foundering" thought. I am myself, without being able to prove my freedom. Objectified it looks like arrogance, or collapses.

Third: I become conscious of my responsibility and freedom simultaneously in a paradoxical manner as a gift. I decide upon my being; I realize myself, and experience myself in this way nevertheless as given to myself, as brought to myself, without being able to say how it happened. That this "coming to myself" is not at my own disposal I experience in the fact that I can also fail, can miss this possibility, can sink into the world in which there is no place for existence. This failure is experienced as emptiness and denial, but the "coming to myself" though as a burden, nevertheless as fulfilment, as grace.

That is revelation for existence. It is not a revelation which merely places me before the boundary of my objective knowledge, that is, before the finitude of my world. This boundary remains immovable as long as nothing other than objective-conceptual thought stands at my disposal for the illumination of existence. Revelation for existence cannot be proved. The relation to Transcendence does not have a merely negative character. It attains positive content here not merely because what cannot be objectively conceived forms the final pole of the relations to Transcendence bound up with the awareness of the boundary, but rather because I experience myself as existence related to Transcendence. This content, of course, cannot be adequately expressed, because existence is not objective. Since I become aware of myself in non-objectified ways as authentic being in responsibility and freedom—and this not as my own creation, but as a gift, so the statements about Transcendence which result from this are statements of faith. For it is just in this way that we see the nature of faith. Faith, as distinct from knowledge, is an awareness of my authentic existence as related to Transcendence, an awareness which is not to be objectively conceived, but can be illuminated in this way only up to the boundary. Just as a consciousness about Transcendence to be illuminated in this way is faith a matter of reason.

From this fact, those speculations, which, on the basis of the thought abstracted from existence, are transgressions of the boundary which are punished with emptiness, attain justification and content. From the standpoint of existence we not only can, but must make statements about Transcendence. Existence knows itself in this freedom not as self-made, but as created, as a creature of a Creator. Since I do not exist merely as existence, but simultaneously as a piece of the world—just that world with which I am indissolubly united, but in which I come to myself—for this reason faith cannot merely speak of itself as creature. For it the world is at the same time also creation. Moreover, in that existence knows itself to be distinguished from the world, it expresses the revelation of Transcendence not only as a revelation of the Creator, but—in view of the special possibility of receiving itself as a gift in the world as existence—as a revelation of the Creator as Redeemer.

With these assertions about revelation for existence, which are to be worked out in a later connection, a further essential shift has occurred in comparison with the scheme of Old Protestant dogmatics from which we began. While we deny for reason, so far as it deals only with conceptual knowledge, a knowledge of God, but not revelation as such—so now for the theology of existence, for which reason includes in itself faith, the sphere of revelation for reason is extended to that which otherwise in theology remains reserved for the supernatural revelation which is grounded in Scripture. Does the theology of existence not thereby become philosophy?

On that point it can certainly be said that we are conscious that the terms Creator and Redeemer do not stem from the sphere of reason, but rather have been taken over from the Christian biblical tradition. Before we enter upon that other question of the relation of the theology of existence and philosophy, therefore, we wish first to consider the Scripture and its application.

3. TRADITION AND EXISTENCE

When we begin to raise questions—quite indifferently, whether philosophically or theologically—, then we stand thereby never at the beginning, but always already within the tradition. In our thought we are formally and materially stamped by tradition. The concepts and forms of thought of which we make use are only in the smallest part our own creation. And even there where new terms and new ways of thought emerge, they are explained and ratified with relation to those already known. There is no completely new beginning, not even materially. With the terms and structures of thought we always take over as well definite conceptions and contents. Even our most personal experiences are determined by that which we have already taken over as a psycho-mental possession. We are heirs, and inherit the new only with the help of what has been given to us. Depth psychology has shown that this is valid to a still stronger degree for the incomparably larger sphere of the unconscious than for the world of consciousness.

This fact of being formed and endowed by tradition is not at our own disposal. We determine neither the place nor the time of our appearance in the stream of tradition. It is not the case, however, that we are only delivered over to the contingency of our situation. The reverse is true also; namely, the tradition has been delivered to us. Unless the unconscious influences the conscious, unless the documents are preserved or rediscovered, unless the spiritual inheritance is understood, these matters are as if absent, as if dead, without language and without influence. Tradition must be understood and appropriated. Every one who understands enacts the interpretation. What the tradition is depends upon the way in which he understands it. This power of the understanding over the tradition is at least as great as the power of the tradition over the understanding. We are certainly determined in our whole Being by tradition; it can be said with equal right, however, that all Being is for us interpreted Being.

Such considerations as we have here employed do not belong to the original nature of understanding and to its actual enactment. What we have here intimated is, to be sure, also understanding; but it is an understanding of understanding, a theory of understanding, a starting point for a hermeneutic. Hermeneutics, however, is not exegesis, but rather preparation and clarification of the understanding in its enactment. In its concrete enactment the understanding does not continually reflect merely upon itself, otherwise it would proceed into infinity without coming to a conclusion. When I understand, that which I have to understand is for me as I understand it. I can certainly be conscious in this act that it is only so for me, and that it can also be understood in still another way. And I shall never think that understanding is complete, for with every act of understanding I win new insights, and everything that is to be understood is inexhaustible. If here we are not merely playing a game, however, there is always by virtue of that understanding an unconditioned judgment in operation which puts an end to the game. The one who understands says not only, "To me it is so," but "It is so." Moreover, he does not say that arbitrarily, as if he could do otherwise. Rather, he says it under the direction of that which is for him the enactment of understanding, valid as a final, unquestionable authority. Without the presupposition of an absolute validity, no understanding is possible. Understanding is always from one standpoint, namely, the standpoint of existence.

This directness of the understanding from existence, to be sure, must also place its own validity again in question, and it is actually placed in question just where in my understanding I deal with the expression and deposit of the self-understanding of existence enacted by others. In order to deal fairly with this self-understanding of others which confronts me in the objects of understanding, I must suspend my judgment, that is, employ my standpoint only as a heuristic principle with which I deal now actually with something over against me in its particularity, and not altogether only with myself and my interpretations. That is the function of historical-critical explanation and exegesis, both of which are indirect, but at the same time derived from the directness of existence, though not absorbed by it. Through the greatest possible elimination of my own subjectivity, the greatest possible objectivity here is to be sought. In contrast to the historicality of existence (*Geschichtlichkeit*) we speak here of historical (*historisch*) research. Here is also the place of the introduction and comprehensive application of all the perspectives, aids and methods which historical-philological science places at our disposal. In this way there is first disclosed to us the whole richness of tradition.

As little as this historical research may be skipped over or neglected, so little can and may the understanding be content with it alone. Through this indirectness of the historical (*historisch*), the directness of the historicality (*Geschichtlichkeit*) of existence must penetrate; it must assimilate into itself history (*Historie*) in its incompleteness, this being fulfilled on a higher plane, namely, as historicality (*Geschichtlichkeit*) of existence. To the extent of that mutual interpenetration of history of research and historicality of existence, existence in each new, transforming appropriation hears out of the tradition the voice of authority. Authority impresses itself upon existence in freedom, in which existence experiences the self-disclosure of authority as a deepened disclosure of itself. That happens in all contemporary pneumatic, existential and theological exegesis of Scripture—so far as it does not abandon the historicality of existence for a supernatural *Heilsgeschichte* construction, as is especially the case in the so-called theological exegesis.

Furthermore, for the theology of existence the definitions within the Old Protestant doctrine of Scripture which
deal with direct and indirect revelation, the authority of
the inspired canon of Scripture and the inner testimony of
the Holy Spirit, attain significance as statements concerning
understanding as such—to be sure, under the abolition of
the supernatural dogmatic restrictions.

Every original understanding of existence is aware of
the directness of the relation to Transcendence. If this
directness is not limited to the prophets and apostles, then
there is no need for special theories of inspiration in order
to explain them. There is here no need for explanation at
all, because the authority of the tradition in which existence becomes conscious of its relation to Transcendence
cannot become an object of a universally valid theory. The
relevant mythological statements about a speaking and
hearing of God are forms of expression of the self-understanding of existence in relation to Transcendence. Moreover, the directness of the hearing of God, as is shown in
the biblical authors, is not independent of the hearer and
his environment. The revelation of Transcendence is never
abstract, but always concretely historical (*geschichtlich*).
The original understanding only guarantees the truth of
the revelation for itself—not in a generally provable way,
but rather unconditionally for itself. It happens through
faith.

On the contrary, it is a matter of indirect understanding
where existence is not concerned with its Transcendence,
but where the tradition of the understanding of that original, direct kind is being dealt with. Without special direct
understanding there is no access. Here, however, in order
to reflect upon the self-understanding of others in its particularity, use is made of the historical understanding with
its suspension of its own standpoint and the objectifying

of perspectives of others. In this way, the Bible—as every historical document—is for us an object of scientific investigation. The never-ending process of scientific explanation and exegesis of such documents, including Scripture, is what we designate indirect revelation. There are disclosed to us in this way meaningful patterns and, in them, possibilities of the self-understanding of existence about which we would otherwise not know.

By virtue of this indirect understanding there occurs, as we have seen, a new directness of understanding. Truth is disclosed to me in a definite historical objectivity, with the result that it becomes authority for me in freedom. My truth comes in an unprovable way out of the truth of others. In this way we see the meaning of the theological practice of speaking of the Word of God in Scripture, a Word which is understood through the inner testimony of the Holy Spirit.

If it has been disputed in theology whether this testimony of the Holy Spirit is bound up with the letters of Scripture or can succeed independently of them, it must be borne in mind in this connection that truth occurs for existence not just anywhere, but always in historical form, in connection with its own contingent tradition. This tradition, however, is never fundamentally finalized, but is appropriated and transformed through existence. As every canon of sacred writings, so also the biblical canon arose finally according to the measure of the experience of the existential significance of the individual documents. By virtue of its power to speak for existence, the canon was subsequently maintained, and, on the basis of the spiritual experience in it, confessional formulations were occasionally made as a testimony for the way this canon has become effective for definite communities. Precisely the self-attesting, transforming appropriation of the canon points, however, to its abiding openness. As little as the normal tradition allows itself to be arbitrarily established for existence, so little can it be defined for all time. Tradition and existence stand in correlation.

With this classification of the understanding of Scripture within a general hermeneutics—a hermeneutics developed certainly from our relation to Scripture—the principal question of the relation of theology, philosophy and science becomes now more urgent.

4.   THEOLOGY, PHILOSOPHY AND SCIENCE

After what has been said previously it will not be surprising if we assert that there exists in principle no difference between our theology of existence and a philosophy which depends upon the same concept of existence. Theology of existence and philosophy of existence have their common point of origin in the reality of existence as that authentic being in relation to Transcendence, which is neither generally provable nor to be objectified mythologically or metaphysically, but which may be perceived only in faith. That does not mean that theology and philosophy of existence have no relation to scientific knowledge on the one hand, and to mythology or philosophical speculation on the other. On the contrary, both become conscious of the special character of existence just at the boundaries of scientific knowledge, in relation to both the whole of Being and the authentic being of existence. In addition, both understand mythological tradition and philosophical speculation, viewed from the perspective of existence, as expressions of the self-understanding of existence and as irreplaceable symbols of the faith for existence. In the critical, positive relation to science and metaphysics lies the principal and pervading common ground of theology and philosophy of existence.

As existential philosophy stands in contrast to every philosophy which thinks it can complete itself as scientific metaphysics in a closed world-picture, so theology of existence denies as an uncritical venture every such philosophy, but also every kind of theology which undertakes something similar on its own basis. For the theology of existence there is no possibility of completing itself as a scientific system. In connection with the criticism made by existential philosophy, theology of existence sees in such religio-philosophical systems an uncritical absolutizing of finite objectivation, and a destruction of the authentic contents of the faith of existence. Theology of existence as a whole is not science, but rather in its essential pronouncements is a matter of scientifically unprovable faith.

Only with the strict preservation of this domain of faith is theology of existence also science. To the extent that it concerns itself in its statements with the sphere of the validity of scientific knowledge, it can and will be nothing other than a science. That is the case in two directions: First, theology of existence is a science, so far as it deals with any objects of nature and history which can be studied. As there, where existence is at stake, it shows science its boundaries, so there where it deals with the legitimate spheres of science, it strives with all helps, for the sake of the most objective conception, to exclude the influence of the subjectivity of existence. What is there indispensable, is here untenable. As there is no objectivity for existence, so existence is in science only subjectivity. Second: theology of existence is conscious that there stands at the disposal of existence for the illumination of its relation to Transcendence nothing but scientific-objective thought, for the simple reason that there is nothing but objective thought. Therefore, theology of existence, where it deals with its authentic sphere, *i.e.* with the statements of existence in relation to Transcendence, formally remains scientific, objective thinking. It is distinguished from science, however, by its content which is not to be ultimately objectified.

By virtue of this formally universal and materially particular use of objective thinking, theology makes its claim to be a science. It is scientific just through the acknowledgment of the material particularity of the scientific, objective thought universally employed by it.

By means of this science, limited only because of the nature of existence, theology of existence distinguishes itself from that theology which believes that it can make statements about God without consideration of the fact that Transcendence is for existence, and therefore understands mythology and metaphysical speculation as objective truth. We are aware that this kind of mythological theology—including some speculative forms—is the principal manner of appearance of theology. We are also conscious of the significance of this mythological theology in view of the transmission of the myths as forms of expression of the self-understanding of existence in history. Theology and philosophy of existence would be poor without the presence of these mythologies and the self-understanding of existence contained in them. Theology and philosophy of existence are dependent for their own realization upon this mythological tradition. However, the acknowledgment of this dependence upon mythological theology for their full self-realization and as a source for symbolic expressions cannot prevent theology and philosophy of existence from dissociating themselves from this kind of theology as something quite different, and from coming into a positive relation to it only through a transforming appropriation of tradition. Mythological or speculative-metaphysical objectivity is directly unacceptable for theology and philosophy of existence, and can become meaningful to them only from the perspective of existence. It is because theology and philosophy of existence have this possibility of understanding and this positive use of mythology and speculation that they are to be distinguished as theology, or philosophy, from mere science.

At this point the question naturally arises, why and how with reference to this common ground of theology and philosophy of existence a distinction is still to be made between the two. From the point of view of a theology which appears to the theology of existence as mythology, the theology of existence must be judged to be a philosophy, and consequently to be the abandonment of theology. Against this view it can only be said that it is the self-limiting of scientific thought and the nature of existence which have caused it to take this course, upon which course alone theology still seems to be possible.

If, however, the same objection is raised from the side of existential philosophy, namely, that with our theology of existence we are dealing no longer with theology, but with philosophy; to that objection it is to be answered that existential philosophy should not hinder theology from doing in its sphere what the philosophy of existence does in its own tradition. Or is it the case that existential philosophy wishes to acknowledge theology only in a form in which it must deny this theology as something foreign and unacceptable to itself? Should not existential philosophy rather rejoice that, in a sphere in which it cannot feel itself so much at home by virtue of the tradition, a transforming appropriation of tradition from the perspective of existence has been begun in a way in which it can recognize itself as a companion? That which the philosophy of existence wishes to accomplish in the much broader sphere of general cultural history (*Geistesgeschichte*)—an area which always stands in the danger of the loss of concrete historicality; it is just this that the theology of existence would like to see as its task in the Church. Just because of the historicality of existence it has no reason to regard its historical place as inferior or to abandon it. On the contrary, greatly indebted to its tradition and historicality, it sees in the Church its vocational setting—a place which, by comparison with the general social situation, is incomparably difficult, but also all the more promising. It is in connection with its conscious decision to stay grounded upon its own specific theological tradition that it makes the claim to be valid as theology rather than philosophy of existence. Theology of existence is philosophy of existence based on a theological tradition which is for it irreplaceable.

It is because of its historicality which it has not chosen for itself that our theology of existence must be developed in the form of a discussion of the main doctrines of Christian dogmatics. It will be shown in this way—to refer back to the beginning of this chapter—that for the theology of existence, theology is not at all dissolved into a new kind of so-called natural theology, but will be a theology of revelation, a theology which is, to be sure, not possible without reason.

The first doctrine in which this can be demonstrated materially is the doctrine of God in relation to His creation.

CHAPTER 2

GOD FOR EXISTENCE

Theology usually deals with God the Creator in three doctrinal subdivisions: God, Creator, Providence. The doctrines of God and Providence are each customarily unfolded under three perspectives, namely: as doctrines of God with reference to His existence (*Dasein*), His nature (*Wesen*) and His attributes; and the doctrine of Providence as the preserving, accompanying and ruling activity of God (*conservatio, concursus* and *gubernatio*).

We shall take up the doctrine of the Trinity first in connection with Christology, although it generally follows the doctrine of the attributes of God except, as occasionally happens in the newer dogmatics, where it is dealt with at the end as the conclusion of the whole system. Also the doctrines of God's eternal decrees and of predestination, which in the old Reformed systems precede the doctrine of creation, we will treat first under the question of redemption. On the contrary, we will follow the tradition when we present the doctrine of man, who belongs also to creation, in connection with the doctrine of salvation, namely, as its presupposition. Also, the doctrine of angels which has its place here in traditional dogmatics we will first meet in Christology.

26

The specific problem in the entire material which is to be considered by us in this chapter is fundamentally determined in the Old Protestant dogmatics by the opposition between natural and revealed theology. This does not surprise us because of our references in the preceding chapter to the intellectual principles of these systems. The distinction between two different ways of knowledge and sources of knowledge takes effect here in this manner, that some statements about God and His relation to the world are regarded as matters of reason, while others are accessible only for faith in the revelation. For example, God's existence and in part even His nature and His preserving activity are regarded as objects of natural theology. But also in the doctrinal elements which depend upon Scriptural revelation the influence of natural theology is felt, as, for example, in the derivation of the attributes of God from a speculative concept of absoluteness, or in the partially deterministic considerations of the doctrine of *concursus*, or in the different attempts to solve the problem of theodicy.

In Neo-Protestantism this whole system of dogmatics became either scientific metaphysics, or a so-called science of faith. Both types of expression of the Neo-Protestant doctrine of God are today rejected by the theology of revelation as natural theology. In order to eradicate every trace of natural theology, the doctrine of God has already been conceived Christologically. However, new problems again grow out of this theology, above all, the question of the reality of evil and the necessity of the saving work of Christ.

For the theology of existence also a doctrine of God is not possible in the form of a science of God and His creation apart from existence, but rather only on the basis of revelation for existence. In distinction to that so-called

Christological theology, there is for it, to be sure, reason itself which becomes aware of the impossibility of the proofs for the existence of God, and it is likewise reason which illumines the relation of existence to Transcendence. In place of the revelation of God in Jesus Christ there appears here first the revelation for existence. What that means we shall realize in what follows in the four problems of the proof of the existence of God, the personality of God, the question of miracle and the problem of theodicy. In this way we attain to the doctrine of God of the theology of existence, corresponding to the *loci* of the Old Protestant dogmatics which included God's existence, God's nature and attributes, Creation and Providence.

1.   THE PROOFS FOR THE EXISTENCE OF GOD AS UNPROVABLE

In dogmatics the so-called proofs for the existence of God are regularly discussed under the perspective of the existence of God. Pre-Kantian theology believed that it was able to see proofs for the existence of God in the syllogistical methods already partially transmitted from ancient philosophy and primarily developed in medieval scholasticism. Since Kant it has become customary to speak principally of four such proofs for the existence of God by natural reason: the ontological, the cosmological, the physico-theological or teleological, and the moral. From the concept of God as the most perfect Being the ontological argument infers His reality. From the conditioned the cosmological infers as Unconditioned as its cause. From the regular and purposeful constitution of the world the physico-theological infers its Author; from the moral consciousness the moral infers God as the Guarantor of a moral world order.

Now it was Kant himself who in his *Critique of Pure*

Reason subjected the first three arguments to an annihilating criticism, and, insofar as he retained the fourth—the moral argument—this is for him not a matter of theoretical, but of practical reason, *i.e.* of the moral consciousness of practical reason. This consciousness is no longer objectifiable, but makes a claim upon the whole personality. Indeed, the proofs for the existence of God as results of objective thought are untenable. God can neither be derived from thought nor proved from the world. The existence of God is no attribute which—as the ontological argument would have it—can be deduced from the concept of God as the most perfect Being. With the category of causality, with which the cosmological argument operates, we do not arrive at Being as such (*Sein an sich*), but remain necessarily stuck in the world of our finite objectivity. Furthermore, the physico-theological argument is guilty of the error that beyond the meaningful in the world, on the basis of which it speaks of God as the Author of this miraculous work, it omits everything which disturbs its harmony and perfection. And also the so-called moral argument leads to illusory postulates which have grown out of a need when its value judgments are applied in the sense of judgments of being.

Under the weight of this critique of rational metaphysics the Neo-Protestant theology, so long as it still speaks of proofs of the existence of God, either withdraws to the so-called religious knowledge of values with which however it goes directly into the arms of Feuerbach, or understands the cosmological proof no longer in the sense of a logical conclusion of discursive thought, but rather as the expression of wonder over the entire non-self-understandable character of existence as it comes to expression in the question which is unanswerable for objective thought; why is there something and not nothing? However, this

astonishing awareness of the contingency of existence offers
no proof of Transcendence; rather, objective thinking arrives at the limits of its knowledge, in which there comes
to consciousness for it the groundlessness of its object-
world. With every statement concerning something beyond the boundary it would disavow this boundary, or
would pull that about which it makes a statement into the
sphere of its finite objectivity. One cannot therefore speak
here of a proof of God, but rather only of a foundering of
objective thinking with reference to what is inconceivable
to it.

We know about this inconceivable sphere not only in
the foundering of objective knowledge upon it, and par-
ticularly, not because of so-called proofs for the existence
of God; rather, that with which we are concerned is for us
with a quite different kind of certainty, and prior to such
undertakings, present in the consciousness of existence that
it is related to Transcendence. In that existence experiences itself as a freedom that is given, it knows in union
with its nature about the reality of its origin, a reality
which is basically different from it, but certainly not to be
separated from it. And in that existence is experienced in
all its character as being removed from the world simultaneously as a piece of the world, its Creator is at the same
time for it the Creator of the world. Existence knows about
this in a manner capable of no proof—in the immediacy of
faith.

And it is just this which is presupposed consciously or
unconsciously in the arguments for the existence of God.
The proofs for the existence of God are not undertaken for
the purpose of discovering something new, previously un-
known, but rather to illumine and to communicate to
others that which one believes he knows. It is thoroughly in
order if we treat them as articulations of faith, as movements of thought in which existence brings to conscious-

ness its relation to Transcendence in its particularity and also in its manifoldness. This can happen of course only with the aid of conceptual-objective knowledge—for we have no other possibility of knowledge—and in objects of our empirical-conceptual world—because there is for us no other object-world. In this way existence can illumine its relation to Transcendence conceptually and objectively, from the various starting-points of individual proofs for the existence of God and in their different ways of thinking.

Such starting-points and ways of thinking are especially: 1) the experienced imperfection of finite existence (*Dasein*) and the conclusion that existence should belong to a perfect Being (in the ontological argument) —2) the experience of the contingency of existence (*Dasein*) and the quest for an Unconditioned (in the cosmological argument) —3) the establishment of the regular and purposeful in the world and the construction of a corresponding all-powerful and all-wise Founder (in the physico-theological argument) —and finally, 4) the knowledge of the ethical norms and the postulation of a Guarantor who makes possible their maintenance and realization (in the moral argument). Precisely in the unattainability of these goals of knowledge for conceptual-objective thinking existence becomes conscious of its unprovable faith. In the concepts of the existence of a perfect Being, of the Unconditioned, of the all-powerful and all-wise Founder, of the Guarantor of the moral order—all unattainable for conceptual-objective thinking—existence now recognizes symbols for the transcendent depths of its imperfection, contingency, determined-ness and ethical obligation. Through the failure of method of proofs those empirico-conceptually conceivable realities become transparent for Transcendence. The unprovability of God becomes for the existence which illumines itself by conceptual-objective thought a "proof" of

God. In that reason is conceptual-objective thinking on the basis of existence, and the ideas of reason are valid only for existence, one can thus speak here of rational proofs of God.

These are the ways in which existence appropriates the traditional proofs of God, assures itself of its faith in the existence of God and can make faith understandable to others. On the contrary, the theology of existence can only deny every proof of God which should consist of something else other than the unprovability of God; for only unbelief wishes to prove God other than in His unprovability. In the history of the arguments for the existence of God faith as well as unbelief have been at work. In what precedes only the existence of God has been discussed. How does it stand now with the possibility of statements about God's nature and attributes?

2.   THE NATURE OF GOD AS PERSONALITY
FOR THE ONE WHO PRAYS

If we could speak of the existence of God in a way not generally demonstrable, but only in the conceptual-objective illumination of the faith of existence, so we must emphasize this basis of faith still more decisively when we come now to deal with statements about the nature and attributes of God. Old Protestant orthodoxy depended for these doctrines—in distinction to that of the existence of God—upon the revelation in Scripture available only to faith. Nevertheless, it made formal as well as material concessions to natural theology, so that its explanations just at these places awaken the impression of disunity and conflict. For the theology of existence, on the contrary, God, as in His existence, so also according to His Being, or nature, and His attributes, is knowable only for existence in faith. From this there results on the one side commonality with, and on the other, contrast to the doctrines of the nature and attributes in the so-called Scripture-theology. This theology of existence also is contrasted with that speculative theology which, for the sake of the purity of the concept of God, prefers to make no statements about the nature and attributes of God—or else regards those definitions which it derives from the concept of the Absolute as statements about the nature of God as such.

For theology of existence a doctrine of the nature and the attributes of God can consist neither simply of a systematizing of biblical statements about God as supernatural revelation nor of the unfolding of the nature of the absolute Spirit in the form of a scientific metaphysics. Out of its self-understanding existence knows of the historicality of all such statements, and the differentiation and contradistinction of the so-called biblical systematizing and philosophical speculations about the Spirit sufficiently confirm this. Because there is a positive revelation of God only for existence, the theology of existence in its statements about the nature and attributes of God is limited by its historicality. But despite the insight into the relativity of such statements, the theology of existence does not believe that it has to give them up completely. In their relationship to existence the formulations of biblical-Christian as well as philosophical doctrines of God in this respect become for it rather possibilities of becoming conscious of its relation to Transcendence in a concrete way and according to all its dimensions. Definitions of the nature and attributes of God present for the theology of existence concrete formulations of its conscious relation to Transcendence. As it is determined by the tradition in which it finds itself, so it interprets this tradition also from the perspective of faith.

In this context, instead of only a sketchy exposition of one such doctrine of the nature and attributes of God, we shall clarify here, at least in reference to an essential, but controversial concept, what is meant *in concreto* with these basic statements, namely in reference to the concept of the personality of God. We may be content with one example because the remaining attributes of God which here stand in question come into play in other connections in the way indicated above.

For the Bible, as is quite self-understandable for mythological tradition, God is simply personality. In the Bible, as is indicated in its beginning, not only is man created in the image of God, but also the image of God carries universal human traits. Here God speaks and hears, feels and rules, gets angry and loves, punishes and shows mercy— quite as a man—and is conceived also with the corresponding organs and limbs. He is a personal being, not an impersonal power or abstract spirit. That is most clearly evident in that one can pray to Him. Prayer as discourse with God in the certainty of being heard and understood by Him and of receiving an answer from Him is quite different from philosophical contemplation in which man has to do only with himself, even if in relation to eternity, or from magic in which one believes that he is able to have at his disposal powers or their personifications. One can pray only to a person who is at the same time not man, that is, to a personal God.

But now the question arises, whether it is possible to pray to a personal God. Are we not concerned merely with a human reflection and magical praxis? Does the concept of personality not offer an inadmissable humanization of God, from which one should detach himself in theology? Over against such arguments others emphasize that the concept of a personal God is necessary for the sake of the ethical and religious personality of man, or indeed, that man only becomes a person in that he knows himself summoned by God.

As worthy as these considerations are—for the reality of

the personality of God for the one who prays they are not
justified. The act of prayer is the directly enacted relation
of existence in its historicality to Transcendence. As such
it is not objectifiable. In that moment where the one who
prays reflects upon his praying, that is, upon the reality
of the personal Other and of the actual existence of the
relation between God and himself, he is no longer praying,
but reflecting upon prayer. As an object of conceptual
knowledge prayer has become something quite different
from what it is in its concrete and actual enactment. No
one wishes to prove where there is nothing to prove—
existence in its actualization is not provable, but rather is
real only in the act of self-actualization, *i.e.* in faith. Therefore all those discussions of the arguments for and against
a personal God in His reality for existence which occur in
the sphere of conceptual-objective thinking can only be
by-passed. While such arguments deal only with objectivations of the relation of existence to God, this relation of
God to existence enacts itself in its utter non-objectivity in
prayer. For the one who prays God is a person in a manner
capable of no proof, but also needing none.

That does not mean that those conceptual-objective discussions of the provability of God would on this account
be unfitting or superfluous. On the contrary: As prayer will
vary, according to whether and what kind of reflection has
preceded it, and as that which is the content of the prayer
hereafter is to be subjected in objective representation to
an examination by conceptual thinking, so the secret of the
personality of God which is real only for existence constantly encompasses conceptual-objective thinking. If out of this
there is not to come an idol, then such critical testing is
indispensable—just so, faith is in turn necessary so that
it does not remain an abstract idea. Only for existence
illumining itself through thought is the idea of the
personality of God a legitimate expression of its relation

to Transcendence. Existence actualizes itself to the degree that in it is illumined in this manner the personal character of its Transcendence.

This is true of other statements about the nature and attributes of God for which the example given here of the personality of God for the one praying may serve as a guide. Instead of further extending this doctrine in this sense, let us turn now to the next, which is concerned with God's Creation.

3.   CREATION AS MIRACLE

That the Old Protestant dogmatics meant by creation not only a unique, settled event in the past, but rather a constant activity of the Creator in relation to His creation is evident from the fact that it spoke in the doctrine of Providence of a *creatio continua* by which God continually preserved His creation and without which it would have had in itself no continuation. Without this expansion of the authentic doctrine of creation through the doctrine of preservation, the danger of deism would threaten—with the expansion the other possibility arose, namely, the merging of God with the powers and laws immanent in the world, thus pantheism, through which the concept of the Creator seems to be called in question. Against both aberrations, the deistic as well as the pantheistic, there stands still another definition of the doctrine of Providence, namely, the concept of the extraordinary intervention of God in the world, with the rescinding of the orders given in it by Him for the purpose of the preservation and confirmation of the creature. For the scientific view of the world there arises at this point the difficulty of the assertion of miracles which signify a rescinding of the laws of nature.

Both problems of the relation of God to the world which come into view here, the problem of creation as a mythical event at the beginning of the world as well as the question of the possibility of miracles, are solved for the theology of existence in this way, that it sees in the relevant opposing assertions—the world as creation or as eternal, faith in miracles or combatting miracles—the consequence of false objectivations and is able to understand creation as a miracle and miracle as creation from the perspective of existence.

For the scientific view of the world there is neither creation nor miracle in the sense of the biblical mythology. For the scientific knowledge of the world, the world is only a never final totality of regular relationships. Only within a horizon ultimately inconceivable for science is scientifically valid knowledge possible. Therefore nothing can be said scientifically about the beginning of the world. To be sure, science can expose the objective understanding of the myths of origin and creation as unscientific; but it becomes a mythology itself when it, in replacing these myths, wishes to make valid statements about the origin of the world. Further it is to be observed that that horizon which hinders the finalizing of the scientific world-picture is in no way fixed, but is movable. The explainability can be extended, even if all is never dissolved in explainability, all the more since suddenly there can appear the unexplainable in the midst of what holds as explained.

In view of this state of affairs the concept of miracle for science coincides with the horizon of the scientifically explainable. Miracles are—scientifically seen—connections which still have to be explained in their causality. The miracle is for science the horizon as such, *i.e.* that reality of which it catches sight when it asks the question: why is there something and not nothing?—the question to which, so far as it deals with the myth of creation, no scientific answer can be given.

With these negative limitations the way is open to speak positively of creation and miracle—no longer in the sphere of scientific thought, but rather in faith from the perspective of existence which can understand and employ mythology as an expression of the understanding of existence.

While science as its extreme possibility can only stand in awe before the fact of existence and essence of the investigable world, but may give no answer to the question of the ultimate origin and purpose, existence speaks here of the Creator and His will. It knows therefore not in the form of provable knowledge from the world, but rather from the awareness of its reception of itself as a gift in freedom—an awareness no longer to be objectified. Therein it expresses itself as creation, and because it is its self-realization which it perceives as created being, so for it the source which it thanks for its existence and essence is not a merely impersonal power, and also not a majority of such anonymous powers, but rather, because of the unity of its own being, a creative personality of which it becomes most expressively aware in prayer. For it this God of existence, because of its indelible involvement in the world, is at the same time the Creator of the world. Thus in the faith of existence the miracle of existence, about which science also knows, becomes the creation of God.

For existence there exists neither the danger of deism nor of pantheism. It understands the miracle of creation not as a single act of the past, but rather as constantly present. But the knowledge of its own creatureliness protects existence from a pantheistic understanding of the relation of God to the world. Although the theology of existence can speak of the Creator not detached from existence and the world, but rather only from the perspective of existence and from this in connection with the world of the Creator, so for it the Creator nevertheless does not coincide with existence or the world, but rather remains unmistakably distinguished from it as "the Wholly Other."

For the theology of existence creation has meaning only

as *creatio continua*; because of this, there is appropriate
for it in all being and occurrence which is seen in the relation of faith to Transcendence the character of miracle.
In consequence of this there is for it no miracle as the
rescinding of the regularities and laws of natural occurrence. It speaks of miracle in a special sense where it has in
mind events which lead to the conclusion that existence
is aware of its special character in the world and is capable
of fulfilling its destiny. As a designation for this special
creative activity of God it claims, beyond the concept of
the Creator, the concept of God as Redeemer — which
stands with the concept of Creator in the biblical-Christian
tradition.

Before we turn to this aspect of a special saving, creative
activity of God, we must deal in the context of the doctrine
of creation with the problem of theodicy which has been
set before us in what was said above. The question is:
how can there be united with God's miraculous preservation of His creation the activity which destroys creation?

4. THE PROBLEM OF THEODICY

Out of the circle of the doctrine of Providence we single
out here the problem of theodicy, because on the one hand
the concept of God's accompanying activity, the *concursus,*
as well as also the thought of the divine rule of the world,
relates to this problem, and because on the other the question of theodicy has belonged at all times to the most burn-
ing religious problems. With reference to the real situation of the world the question is actually posed whether
God, as its Creator, may be held simultaneously to be all-
powerful and infinitely good. How can the evil in the
world be reconciled with the rule of an all-powerful and
infinitely good God?

The definitions of the Old Protestant dogmatics about
the accompanying and ruling activity of God are formula-

tions of the problem rather than a solution of it. For
either God's overall activity is limited for the purpose of
releasing Him from the authorship of evil, or the question
under consideration is rejected for the unfathomable maj-
esty of the divine activity as such. The doctrine of Last
Things, in consequence of which God will judge the world
justly and will consummate His creation, first brings the
actual solution. As a demonstration of the final glory of
God, somewhat wider scope seems to be given to the devil
in God's first creation, and in view of this activity of the
anti-divine powers too much is expected of faith in God's
providence which already makes itself evident.

It is thus understandable that also in theology ideas of
inner-worldly processes of development and progress again
and again emerged, in consequence of which the evil in
the world is progressively overcome, or that it presents only
a phenomenon to be exposed in an intellectual-theoretical
manner—a phenomenon that does not belong to Being as
such. If in the former there is the view of the Last Judgment, which justifies God, so in the latter it is the conception of God as a spiritual power operating in all and con-
quering, which expels the evil and bad from the world.

Over against this optimism of believing trust or of appeal to the outer or inner activity men appeared again and
again who for the sake of the reality of evil in the world
denied the reality of a good God, attempted too much in
speculations about a God who is becoming, or saw the
final conclusion in the acknowledgment of the unfathomableness of God's wisdom. However, as for faith in God
the absurd becomes a riddle, so for atheism the meaningful in the world. Agnosticism, however, which acknowledges both and would like therefore to speak of the ground
and abyss of Being and of meaning in God, must be asked
in what sense its statement is meant: whether it is dealing

with a universally valid statement or with a confession of faith for existence. In both cases, nevertheless, we would have to do not merely with the unfathomableness of God; for a scientifically established unfathomableness is no longer final unfathomableness—at least then science, which establishes this statement, would be excepted from it—and an unfathomableness for existence is quite different from mere unfathomableness.

With this we have reached the point from the perspective of which there is given to the theology of existence the possibility and necessity of taking a position with reference to the whole problem of theodicy outlined here and to its attempts at a solution. Theology of existence, over against this whole complex of problems, must in the first place draw attention to the distinction between objective-scientific statements, mythological-speculative ones and those valid for faith from the perspective of existence.

The statements which lead to the problem of theodicy are made in the sphere of universally valid, conceptual-objective knowledge. In our spatio-temporal experiences and in the experiences conceived in the categories of our understanding the absurdities are established, and for our rational thought which tends to unity are produced the tensions and ununitable elements in the concept of God. The establishing of these contradictions is thoroughly in order, so long as we are conscious that we are operating in the sphere of conceptual-objective knowledge. We have at our disposal no other possibilities and methods for the illumination of our situation in the world and of those formulations in which others before us conceived the results of these conceptual illuminations and in which we conceive them today.

The theology of existence however acknowledges not merely the appropriateness of the questions and makes them its own; rather, just as much it must now show the limits of such questions and answers. The "world as a whole" is for science a border-concept, beyond which it can make no further statements. The speculative concept of the "world as a whole" or the mythological picture of the creation of God corresponding to it are no longer scientifically provable statements, but are the expression of the consciousness of the relation of existence to Transcendence. The same holds true, as we have indicated, for the so-called attributes of God: omnipotence and infinite goodness. In them we are not dealing with a scientific description of the nature of God, but rather with symbols of the faith for existence.

In this, not the formation and discussion of the problem of theodicy in the context of scientific knowledge, but its solution in this context is acknowledged as unfeasible and misplaced. If Christian belief in *Heilsgeschichte* or philosophical speculation about the spirit (*Geist*); if atheism or agnosticism are taken for scientifically provable objectivity instead of as forms of expression of the relation of existence to Transcendence, then there can appear only assertions which are untenable and easily to be refuted. The faith in the *heilsgeschichtlich* consummation then necessarily becomes mere mythology, the spirit-speculation becomes unreal phantasy, atheism and agnosticism become contradictions in themselves.

It is otherwise, however, with the alleged solutions to the problem of theodicy when we do not see in them dogmas of faith raising the claim to universal validity or results of science, but rather movements of thought of the faith of existence in its contemporary historical situation—movements which are concretized in mythological and speculative symbols. So understood, the mythology of the *Heilsgeschichte* which leads from the Fall and the rule of demons to the Last Judgment and the New Creation can be believed as an answer to the question of the evil and bad in God's world. Because this faith for existence, however, cannot be absolutized, so it will become open for the truth of the rule of the spirit over nature contained in the different spirit-speculations and of the inner freedom of the spirit from the world—all the more since the Logos speculation in the Christian tradition has been connected from early times with the biblical *Heilsgeschichte*. But even atheism as the legitimate protest against every abso-lutizing of a finite objectivation can be understood as an expression of the faith of existence. Only it must be protected from the absolutizing of its own negation through the acknowledgment of an unfathomableness of God—whereby this may be understood not in the sense of an agnosticism which absolutizes itself again, but rather only may be taken as a statement of the existential consciousness of existence.

The answer of the theology of existence to the problem of theodicy does not consist accordingly in a theory, but rather in an interpretation of the different mythological and speculative attempts to solve the problem from the perspective of the self-understanding of existence. The criterion for employing one or the other expression is for it the manner in which thereby a clarification of existence in relation to Transcendence becomes possible. This clarification remains for it, however, not a mere theory of the relation of God to the world or of the world to God. Rather, as for the theology of existence God as a whole is only for existence, so its theodicy holds good finally only on the way to the self-actualization of existence. Where this becomes possible for existence, redemption occurs. Of this we shall speak in the next chapter under the title: Existence as Grace.

CHAPTER 3

EXISTENCE AS GRACE

In the Old Dogmatics the doctrine of salvation usually comprises three parts: *Anthropology*, in the form of the original state of man, the Fall and original sin as the presuppositions of salvation; *Christology*, that is, the doctrine of the person and work of the Redeemer as the realization of salvation; and, *Soteriology* as the doctrine of the realization of the redemption of the sinner through justification and sanctification.

Since the time of its origin in the Reformation, Protestant dogmatics has dealt in these doctrines with the antitheses of law and works, or gospel and grace, self-redemption or redemption from without, and a mythological-magical or spiritual-personal understanding of redemption. Over against the Catholic synergism of nature and grace, the Reformers—corresponding to their own experience and on the basis of their understanding of Scripture—stressed salvation as a pure gift of grace of the saving act of God which happens in Christ for faith. The believer is not made righteous, not prepared for good works by sacraments which operate magically; rather, as a sinner, he is declared righteous in faith in the forgiving love of God in Christ. In order to exclude every kind of human cooperation in redemption and to make certain of its character as pure grace, the doctrines of original innocence and the Fall were intensified in this respect, namely, that for man after the Fall the original perfection is missing, with the result that he can in no way co-operate with the divine activity of grace. The doctrine of grace already caused the Reformers and their direct descendants many kinds of difficulties, partly in its practical effects, partly in its scriptural basis. The conflicts over the doctrine of justification on the Lutheran side and the doctrine of predestination on the Reformed side bear clear witness to this fact. Already in the confessional formulations and the systems of Old Protestant Orthodoxy the much exaggerated formulations of natural man's total involvement in sin, the sole activity of grace and man's being merely declared righteous by virtue of the saving work of Christ have been greatly attenuated.

To a later generation, with a different, more positive conception of the capacities of natural man and with a correspondingly different understanding of the historical appearance of Jesus, the Old Protestant doctrine of salvation must appear as a magical salvation from without, and therefore, to a degree exactly that kind of salvation which the Reformation in its rejection of sacramentalism had itself denied. In continuity with the Reformation and on the basis of a better understanding of Scripture, Neo-Protestantism thought it could withdraw the doctrine of salvation from the controversy over nature and grace, law and gospel, and see in it the principle of a more deeply Christian general religiosity, and Christ as its archetypal actualization.

In this way Neo-Protestant theology attained, to be sure, a doctrine of sin and justification which, to a theology which is again strongly aligned with the Reformation, must appear as a works-righteousness and a self-redemption which does not take seriously enough the reality of sin. That there can be no simple return to the Reformation is evident from the fact that in this theology the problems again emerge with which the Reformation concerned itself in its own time and which in the aftermath led beyond its position. The interest with which the Catholic theology encounters this renewal of Reformation theology proves clearly that its substantial relationship with Catholicism is much greater than in Neo-Protestantism, greater in any case than the Catholicizing tendencies of which this Neo-Reformation theology in another regard accused Neo-Protestantism.

In the doctrine of redemption, as in the other doctrines, the theology of existence is concerned not primarily with this complex opposition of Catholicism and Protestantism, but with the validation of those elements of the Christian tradition which appear relevant for a redeeming self-understanding of existence. From its concept of existence it develops therefore the concept of sin, and from this perspective seeks to understand the dogma of original innocence, the Fall and original sin. Likewise from the self-understanding of existence it unfolds the nature and reality of justification and sanctification in order to gain access to the doctrine of election from this perspective. There are not only external reasons which cause it in this understanding of existence as grace at first to disregard Christology and later to devote a special chapter to it. This postponing of Christology, as will be shown later, is rather based on the material itself. Existence can also be understood as grace independently of Christology, even though later, for the sake of our historical situation, a Christology

of existence will be shown to be indispensable. To begin
with, we must deal here with sin and grace apart from
Christology.

1. THE NATURE OF SIN

Sin is no fact which can be established and proven with
universal validity. What can be designated as sin are only
the breaches of legal rules and moral commandments. Such
laws and rules are based on natural, political, ethical and
religious orders of value. So-called natural law, political
ordinances, traditional *mores* and public morals, the ethos
which comes to expression in individual conduct and lives
in a community, that which is valid in religion as a code
—these are such orders of value. Whoever transgresses them
is guilty before these tribunals and, to be sure, in a manner
that the fact of guilt as well as its extent can be generally
proven.

Just in this objectivity of their norms and in the universal validity of their judgments, however, these ordinances are at the same time relative, equivocal and vari-
able, and naturally place themselves partially in question.
They are relative because they are always related in their
objectivity to a definite order which as such is not the only
one, nor always the same. Even natural law has a history
and requires interpretation. This is true to a still greater
degree of political institutions and social structures. A sub-
jective element is always present in the demand for justice.
Even the codified divine commandments are not applied
unequivocally, but admit of different interpretations.
Moreover, the individual orders of value stand in compe-
tition with one another and very often conflict with each
other. Natural law and current law, as well as current law
and moral consciousness, worldly and spiritual law can
oppose each other. Whoever obeys one will be guilty there-

by of the other; what appears under one definite aspect as absolutely correct, has to be judged from another point of view as grave guilt. The guilty remain here unpunished, and the innocent are judged.

These variations and conflicts of value show that there is in this sphere no absolute validity. Transgressions and feelings of guilt which attend them are certainly generally provable, but are relative for just this reason.

And yet something absolute already appears in this relativity of objectively conceivable orders of value and possible violations of them. This unconditional element lies in the fact that these orders of value exist at all, and that there is for man no possibility of exempting anything from them, therefore of isolating a value-free or value-neutral sphere in which one does not have to decide. All that we do and everything at our disposal is for us in some way useful or harmful, right or wrong, good or evil. In this inescapability of choice, evaluation and decision, something absolute appears in all the ambiguity and relativity. This is evident in the fact that this situation of unavoidable decision can no longer be objectified and proven as universally valid. If I wish to prove to myself and others that it is I who here decide, then the situation of unlimited decision dissolves into limitedness and arbitrariness, or even slavery. Whatever is decided in all objectively establishable limitations and dependencies in freedom—that is existence.

Here we are finally at the place where we can discuss sin and unconditioned guilt as distinguished from mere transgressions and relative guilt-feelings. Only existence is able to know of sin and, correspondingly, of guilt in an authentic sense. Existence cannot fulfil or transgress something; rather, it fulfils or fails itself. For existence, *this* or *that* thing is not merely good or evil; rather, existence is itself good or evil. There is sin only before God in faith. Existence, however, knows itself to be related to God. In this relation it understands the voice of God in the relative objectivations of the orders of value of its historicality in a non-objectifying, limited way.

How the voice of God speaks for existence depends upon the following: the kind of tradition in which it stands, the concept of natural law one has, the kind of political legislation under which one lives, the kind of moral concepts and divine commandments he knows, and the manner in which he conceives all these orders of value and intelligibly illumines them, the kind of experiences he has with them, and finally, the way he has permitted himself to be determined by them in his conduct up to the present. What existence hears as the voice of God when it awakens to itself, becomes aware of its freedom and responsibility, accepts its historicality unconditionally and knows itself therein as related to Transcendence—what it hears is again objectified, brought into relationship, tested, discussed and therewith divested of its absoluteness. In that non-objectifiable reception of oneself as a gift in freedom, however, one is able to hear the absolute in the objectivity of historical orders of value, and my transgression of what is understood as an absolute demand becomes sin.

In this way the traditional doctrines of the Fall and of original sin gain their significance as a presupposition for the understanding of existence as grace.

2. THE SIGNIFICANCE OF THE DOCTRINES OF THE ORIGINAL CONDITION OF MAN, OF THE FALL AND OF ORIGINAL SIN

The Old Testament story of the Fall and its interpretations by the Apostle Paul (Romans 5) cannot be regarded either naturally or supernaturally as objective pronouncements about the beginning of human history. Regarded naturally, they lead to a theory of development which is not verifiable and which—as far as scientific investigation is possible—is a false theory of human development. Death cannot be spoken of scientifically as the wages of sin. If the stories are treated supernaturally, that is, understood as the initial element in a supernatural *Heilsgeschichte*, human responsibility for sin (in opposition to the Bible) is placed in question, as the discussions of the dogma show.

The meagre biblical intimations concerning the condition of man before the Fall can most easily be understood in the sense of a biographico-historical pronouncement, in so far as man, before he is awakened to his nature as existence, knows—just as Adam and Eve in Paradise—authoritatively delivered prescriptions about what is permitted or forbidden, but does not actually know of sin and guilt. So regarded, the story is concerned neither with a situation which once existed at the beginnings of human history, nor with a condition which—as dogma has it—can be described as original perfection. This "state of innocence" exhibits no positive property which one could to any degree forfeit, but deals simply with that non-differentiation which is characteristic of man prior to his awakening to consciousness and which, among the miseries which this awakening causes him, he can remember sometime as a lost innocence. From the perspective of existence, however, the so-called original state simply signifies that childlike existence in which is found the one who has not yet awakened to the consciousness of his situation as existence and to which he can never return once this consciousness has dawned.

In this same way is determined the meaning of the myth of the Fall from the perspective of existence. For existence, the Fall means not the loss of an alleged perfection about which the Bible knows nothing in a dogmatic sense, but rather positively the movement from non-existential innocence into the knowledge of the existence of good and evil and—simultaneously—of sin and guilt. The temptation by the snake which is connected with this apparent progress consists in the fact that man can mistake this knowledge of good and evil for a divine likeness and at the same time evade the responsibility enclosed therein. The tree whose fruit facilitated this knowledge itself belongs to God's creation, and when the myth wishes to protect man from the consequences of partaking of the fruit, it only expresses the metaphysical tragedy which lies enclosed in the being of existence for man—without however absolutizing the element of tragedy and removing the human guilt.

As the myth of Genesis 3 describes it in a uniquely appropriate manner, the Fall has a two-fold dimension: One, if one catches sight of what he is, namely, existence, this can only happen with the result that he puts his material world at his own disposal in conceptual objectivations like a god. Only in this way can he know the world and illumine his nature as existence. But if he persists in this situation, he inverts his true nature with which he had contact into its opposite and falls victim to the world which he seems to have won and to rule. To this pertains the second factor which the myth likewise indicates, namely, that through his objectivation he conceals from himself the responsibility as existence of which he caught sight through this clarification, and seeks for a cause of his action outside himself. The weird chain of causes, in which there is no personal responsibility, but the blame is put on others, becomes for him at the same time both protection and fate, and disguises itself in the inexplicable fact of the shame—they made aprons for themselves—ineradicable evidence of the responsibility of existence which knows about Transcendence, that is, that stands before God. Here death

becomes the wages of sin, since for existence its total finitude and, above all, its mortality stands under the sign
of the defection which is necessarily connected with its
coming to itself.

The inescapability and inexcusability of this sinful existence, which appears not only in individual acts, but deter-
mines the whole character of existence in its nature, is what
is meant by the dogma of original sin. For the theology of
existence, this dogma is not concerned with a natural or
supernatural condition, but is rather a mythological expression for the self-understanding of existence. In the concept of original sin the fate-like character of existence as
sin is evident from the fact that it is qualified by sin not
only in its evil, but also in its good conduct. The consequence of evil conduct is the perception of the responsibility through conceptual, illuminating thought in the
context of the concealment and false excusing of the evil
behavior through the same objectifying thinking. Such a
consequence is expressed in the uneasiness and anxiety of
human life, and in the inhumanities which necessarily follow from the same self-assertive attempts motivated by care
and anxiety. Since only man can experience care and anxiety by virtue of his possible, but defective character as existence, so only man can be inhumane. The nature of original
sin, however, also appears in his good conduct, that is, in
every act in which man does not flee his responsibility, but
chooses and decides in the consciousness of his freedom. It
is evident in the unavoidable value-conflicts in which ethical thinking finds itself, from which we cannot escape, but
in which we necessarily become involved anew in every
act. There is for existence no unequivocal good; rather, the
more sharply and successfully it thinks, the more unavoidable the situation of conflict becomes. Thus we of necessity incur guilt with every action or failure to act.

Neither what has been said here about evil nor about good actions of man has been said in the sense of a universally valid scientific anthropology. Such an anthropology does not catch sight of the nature of evil at all. Our statements hold good only for the self-understanding of existence which is not directly conceivable scientifically, and for the enactment and co-enactment of thinking based on existence. We cannot speak here finally of a tragedy of man nor of a tragedy in God, even though this is what must necessarily follow from an objective perspective which disregards existence. For existence sin possesses metaphysical character in that it exhibits a quality of its relation to Transcendence. In the tragic understanding of the self or of God, however, the ground of existence is already lost by virtue of its perspective and self-assertion. The terms "tragedy" and "tragic" can probably contribute conceptual illumination to this situation, but they cannot and may not be the final word. The final word can only be the myth of grace and election which is understood from the experience of a new being of forgiveness.

3. THE JUSTIFICATION OF THE SINNER IN FAITH

The Reformation doctrine of the justification of the sinner by faith alone apart from works of law has already been much discussed in theology and has caused endless mischief. Endless controversial theological and interconfessional discussions have been kindled by this dogma. It represents a resultant stage in the long history which this doctrine, since it was formulated by the Apostle Paul in Romans, has had in Christianity. Colossal ingenuity has been employed to render conceivable why and how the sinful world was redeemed by the saving act of God in the death of His Son on the Cross and can live in the light of a new, perfected creation. It may be a clear sign of the lack of the experience of salvation and the inability to appropriate the experience of others, when in the manifold history from the most divergent phenomena the witness of a grace which is really experienced can no longer be heard. But in view of the objectivizing and absolutizing of the doctrine, in which this consciousness of salvation has been expressed continually, it is understandable that contemporary existential philosophy has felt compelled to regard the dogma of justification as the most absurd and unreliable formulation of the Christian faith.

To the extent that the theology of existence is historically determined by this whole Christian ideological and conceptual world and apart from its being so determined would not speak of sin and grace—to that extent it is conscious that as theology of existence it is not based on these objectivations of a *Heilsgeschichte,* but on its own understanding of existence. Just as certainly as it as an expression of such self-understanding is co-determined in its *fides qua* by the *fides quae* of the tradition, so it understands the traditional *fides quae* only from the perspective of the *fides qua* of its own existence. In the light of this fact we will proceed in our doctrine of justification not from the perspective of the traditional conceptuality of this doctrine, but from the self-understanding of existence as sin which was developed previously.

The self-understanding of existence is not exhausted by its recognition of itself as sinful; rather, in the knowledge and recognition of its relation to Transcendence determined by sin is contained conjointly the clue to a decisively new self-understanding. Existence is no longer merely sinful when it knows itself to be under the power of sin in all its manifestations and does not resist the knowledge, but accepts itself to be that which it knows itself to be. In sin as that desire to be like God produced by objectifying knowledge of good and evil, it takes upon itself responsibility and freedom, and this perversion of its nature expresses itself in care, anxiety and inhumanity. With the recognition of its pervertedness, existence regains its lost responsibility and freedom. The acceptance of itself as a sinful perversion of its destiny is an act of its responsibility and freedom. In the act of becoming aware of the loss of its authentic being, existence affirms itself in its most authentic nature as responsibility and freedom which are not to be objectified.

It should be remembered in this connection what also Reformation theology—in false objectivation, to be sure— established as that remainder of the divine image in the nature of man which was not destroyed or lost, and what it established upon it as _ordo salutis,_ as a way of justification, reconciliation and sanctification of the sinner by means of divine grace. For existence, however, it cannot be a matter of such a quantitatively demonstrable remainder of the _imago Dei_ and a related synergism of human will and divine grace. Existence knows itself in its self-acceptance as sin rather as both completely fallen and completely restored to itself, as completely knowing and deciding, and at the same time as completely known and accepted, completely as freedom and completely as gift—as a new creation. Only in such mutually exclusive paradoxical totalities of sinful existence and existence upon which grace has been bestowed may existence illumine for itself in objectifying "illumination" this comprehensive change, this experience of being placed in a new light.

That I do not have to perish as sinner before the Holy God, that this fire does not annihilate me, but rather that I experience in it, like Isaiah in his famous vision in the Temple (Isa. 6), the purifying power of the divine presence and the call to His service—just this is the grace of a new creation. It is just from such an experience of the "new reception of oneself" in the fire of God that existence first learns what creation is. That is not a matter of the creation of Being as such, that is, the answer to the question, why is there something, rather than nothing, which question existence may afterward provide from such experience; rather, here we find ourselves in the most inner sanctuary of that secret of creation, from which alone we can speak stammeringly of grace. Existence is grace.

The concepts which the Old Lutheran dogmatics in its doctrine of the appropriating grace of the Holy Spirit used for describing the salvation of the sinner through justification and renewal prove to be inadequate; but for illumination they are indispensable attempts to articulate the wonder of the grace of the new creation. It is these concepts of justification and reconciliation apart from works of law—which concepts stem from legal and cultic spheres—that express the metaphysical significance and the special quality of this relation to Transcendence of the new consciousness of existence. It is not existence which here in the enactment of its self-understanding justifies and reconciles itself; rather, it experiences its self-acceptance as it is, as a "being accepted" by God, its "being reconciled with itself" as a "being reconciled with God." There is no trace of its own merit, for the creature is certainly not its own creator.

This same observation is valid also for the confirmation of justification and reconciliation in conversion and sanctification. Conversion means being freed from the state of being "enmeshed" in the world of the objective, a state which engenders care and anxiety. Sanctification as relationship to God consists in the fact that the experienced acceptance and reconciliation of existence is extended to its own generation and environment. But just as little as our being reconciled with the world and man, our being freed from care and anxiety and gaining the capacity for love is something secondary which must be added to justification and reconciliation in faith (as if justification and reconciliation could occur without conversion and sanctification!); so little can we speak of a work of faith with respect to this conversion and sanctification. If objectified as activity and proof of faith, justification by faith would be annulled, because existence would fall again into the sin of objectivation for the purpose of putting the whole matter at its own disposal. Grace and proof of faith existing independent of faith radically exclude each other. Only for existence do conversion and sanctification become perceptible as symbols of grace. It is for this reason that even the Old Reformation *syllogismus practicus*, the manifest correspondence between divine election and the conduct of the elect, is at least a questionable formulation, because here universally valid proof and certainty of election approach one another too closely. This objection holds also for the dogma of predestination, in which the concern of the specifically Lutheran doctrine of justification was treated on the Reformed side. In conclusion we shall treat this dogma, because—when correctly understood—it is quite appropriate for expressing the consciousness of existence as grace.

4. THE EXISTENTIAL CONSCIOUSNESS OF ELECTION

The aberrations which were produced especially by Calvin and his followers by means of the doctrine of predestination are certainly no less great than those which the doctrine of justification produced. As in the latter, which concerned itself with law and gospel, the necessity or pernicousness of good works was contested; so in the discussions of the dogma of predestination positions were reached in which God became the author of evil and man became the characterless tool of blind fate. In both of these positions the cause of these "dead-ends" and monstrosities lies in the perversion of statements of faith for existence into universally valid proof of understanding and its systematizing. That in both of these doctrines something else is being dealt with other than such aberrations is shown in the fact that they often in the course of their history have been genuine expressions of the consciousness of experienced grace, and also in the fact that they can be corrected and understood in this way from the perspective of our understanding of the nature of existence. As we have spoken of the justification of the sinner under this aspect, we must now also interpret the dogma of predestination from the perspective of the consciousness of existence as grace.

In his existence as justified sinner the believer knows that he is elected by God. Election—even radically understood in the sense of the mythology of the double predestination of election and rejection as it is already presented by Paul in Romans 9-11 and after him by Calvin and extreme Calvinism—offers for existence the most adequate expression for the sinner's experience of the reception of himself as a gift in grace. For existence knows about this dark background of the possibility of rejection by the fact that this reception of itself as a gift is not inevitable. It knows therefore that this grace is something completely unmerited, and that its participation in it does not lie in the power of the creature, but exclusively in that of the Creator. On the one hand, it knows positively only of this possibility of being elect, though for it as existence the rejection is already an impossibility, since it would otherwise not be what it is, namely, existence as grace. On the other hand, this possibility of being elect, which excludes that impossibility, stands as a reality only to be believed, and not to be objectified. God is none other than the one who elects it. For existence God is not the one who rejects.

Seen from the perspective of existence, the doctrine of double predestination, wherein without their own will one is destined by God for eternal salvation and the other for eternal damnation, is the consequence of an inappropriate objectivation and absolutizing of intellectual projections. While these projections can be utilized for the illumination of the secret of grace, they may not be absolutized in this objectified form as metaphysical statements. It is certainly a logical conclusion for the understanding, that if God is almighty, both evil and unbelief must be caused by Him. But this practice of coming to a logical conclusion on the part of the understanding stands in its enactment as in its result in greatest contradiction to the revelation of God for existence in faith. Whoever thinks he is able in this manner to come to legitimate statements about the nature of God, has either failed to grasp what existence is, or does not take into account the possibilities and boundaries of objective knowledge. It is not surprising that he attains to a picture of God which not only has nothing to do with the saving God of faith, but stands in irreconcilable contradiction to the consciousness of responsibility on the part of existence. God as author of evil on the one hand, and human responsibility and guilt on the other, are incompatible with one another. Logical determinism and personal freedom radically exclude each other. That the one who argues logically is aware of the impossibility of his position is clear from the fact that he attempts in every way possible to absolve God from the guilt of evil caused by Him and to pass it on to man. These attempts to absolve God, as author of evil, from guilt by means of conceptual-objective thought, and to make man responsible for it are utterly hopeless, just as the whole course of development, whose result makes this sophistry afterwards necessary, is utterly perverted. Objective thinking can only break down before

the boundary of Transcendence and existence. These speculations concerning God as the author of evil and the corresponding arguments which serve only to exonerate God
and burden men shatter in their consequences and contradictions; at best we can see in them the truth of existence in relation to Transcendence as grace which is not
objectively conceivable. Because these theories wish to be
regarded as valid truth in a directly objective way rather
than in a way in which they are self-cancelling and thus so
for that which becomes transparent non-objectively, they
can only be rejected as inappropriate and absurd by a
thinking which knows of existence as grace.

From the perspective of the logical conception of God
as the author of evil, the objection can be raised against
the existential understanding of God as the one who elects
to salvation, that here evil no longer possesses any metaphysical reality and the possibility of being rejected is not
taken into account. This objection is unjustified because
existence is quite aware, even in its relation to Transcendence, of the reality of sin and guilt, and of the angry will
of the God who rejects. But for existence the will and
activity of God are not two separate aspects operating independently of each other. Such an objectivation would
be false, no longer illuminating, but obscuring the reality
of existence. From the perspective of existence the mytho-
logico-speculative conceptions of the two wills of God—
an electing and a rejecting, a concealing and a revealing of
God—are inseparable. Because existence knows itself as
sinful to be entangled in care, anxiety and inhumanity,
and acknowledges itself to be sinful, it is also aware that
it is justified and accepted by God in a new act of creation
and elected to a new being of freedom from the world and
of capacity to love. Otherwise than in this unity of being
rejected and elected it would not have to do with God, but
rather with conceptual distinctions of its objectively il-

luminating thought. As necessary as these conceptual-objective distinctions are for the knowledge of sin and guilt, grace and forgiveness, so much so is the adequate mythological expression for the self-understanding of existence not the God who elects one and rejects the other, but the God who is in one act rejecting and electing. As existence knows itself both rejected and elected, so God is for existence both the one who rejects and who elects. In no other way can it speak of God, or know of sin and guilt—or of grace. For the believer, rejection is the continuing dark background of the election to existence as grace, but he cannot concede more to evil than its being this dark background. The metaphysical quality of its being is just this, that it is chosen by God.

Our interpretation of the doctrine of predestination exhibits a surprising relatedness to the so-called Christological concept of the dogma as is represented today by Karl Barth. The small difference, but one not to be overlooked, consists in the fact that the theology of existence does not once take refuge in a mythological construction to overcome that fateful mythology of the eternal election and rejection by God, as well as the fate of the two different classes of men, and therewith the divine authorship of evil and the deterministic lack of human freedom. Barth's recourse is to the myth of the fulfilment of the rejecting will of God in the fate of His Son. We arrive at our understanding of existence as an election to grace without such mythological aids, but rather directly out of the self-understanding of existence. That does not mean, however, that there is no place for a Christology in theology or that it could dispense with it. But, as for the theology of existence, the doctrine of predestination is an expression of the self-understanding of existence, so Christology for it can only be the expression for this predestinarian self-understanding of existence, namely, Christology of existence.

CHAPTER 4

CHRISTOLOGY OF EXISTENCE

The figure of Christ stands in the center of Christian preaching. There is no Christianity without Christ—neither historically nor confessionally. As Jesus stands at the beginning of Christianity, so every Christian theology has some kind of Christology, that is, a doctrine of the person and work of Christ. This trait which connects all theologies at the same time also separates them. The fact of so many different types of Christian faith and Christian theology is closely connected with the fact that there have appeared in the course of history so many diverse concepts of the nature and significance of Jesus of Nazareth and his mission. In the variations of Christology are reflected the variations in the history of theology.

The Reformers took over without essential modification the Christological dogma of the divine-human Redeemer personality of Christ as it had been a general Christian possession since the Council of Chalcedon (451 A.D.). The discussion of Christology in Reformation and post-Reformation theology took place completely within the context of the previous discussions of the dogma. The new element added to traditional Christology by virtue of the Reformation does not consist so much in the definitions of the nature of the presence of the Exalted Lord in the Sacrament of the Lord's Supper as in the formulation of the doctrine of the three-fold saving work of Christ: namely, the prophetic, priestly and kingly. This doctrine of the three offices of Christ forms the substitute for the Roman concepts of the sacramental presence and the papal representation of Christ denied by the Reformers.

The Chalcedonian Christology, which Old Protestantism held in common with the Roman Catholic Church, and what is added to it was dissolved only in the newer Protestantism. This action applied equally to the doctrines of the person of Christ as to his work. Only the human personality of the historical Jesus remained of this divine-human Redeemer. Suprahistorical divine quality was ascribed to this figure only in so far as through him the supratemporal truth of the Christian principle has entered into history, or through him one can have a special redemptive experience of God's holy love for sinners. The saving work of Christ consists in the introduction of this principle, that is, in making possible this experience of redemption. Of the three offices, only the prophetic remains, while the priestly and kingly can be spoken of only figuratively.

In our time this "modern" Jesus of the completed religiosity has been recognized by the religio-historical and New Testament research as a product of the thinking and feeling of these same modern men. This "Jesus" has less in common with the real Jesus than did the God-man of dogma. Orthodox and liberal theologians of today are in agreement that Jesus lived in the eschatological world of his own time, an ideological world quite opposed to the spirit of the present time; and also, that early Christianity saw in him the supra-earthly Messiah who would come in the imminent judgment of the world. The evaluations of

the worth and significance of this eschatological Jesus, however, are completely opposed to one another. Following
Albert Schweitzer, the newer liberal theology sees in the
primitive Christian eschatology the temporally conditioned
expression of a timeless ethic of culture, and in Jesus the
bearer and embodiment of the same. The tragedy of his
historical activity consists in the fact that he held firm not
to his ethics, but to his concepts of the end-time in which
he was deceived. On the orthodox side, to the contrary, the
appearance of the eschatological perspective led to a renewal of the theology of *Heilsgeschichte*, in that the biblical eschatology was used as a scheme for understanding the
whole course of history, and the God-man was viewed as
its mid-point and as the one who would bring it to completion. As in theological liberalism, alongside a rational
ethical understanding of Jesus a positive evaluation was
made of New Testament eschatology—this being understood, to be sure, as mythology—, so also in orthodox theology the *heilsgeschichtlich* understanding is not unequivocal, but oscillates between an axiological-demythologiz-
ing interpretation and one that is teleological-mythological.
These alternatives are also reflected in the conceptions of
the person and work of the Redeemer.

From the structure of the Christological problem in past
and present as just outlined the following two questions
emerge for every discussion of the problem about the
Christ: First, the question of the relationship of the in-
herited God-man Christology to the newly discovered
eschatological Christ. Here we are dealing with an historical, scientific question, the answer to which is of significance, however, for the relation of Christology and existence. The second question concerns the legitimacy of the
eschatological claim to Messiahship historically conceded
to Jesus. Was Jesus really what he claimed to be and as

what his disciples revered him, namely, God's Son, the Messiah, the King of the End-time—or merely a man who in a human way made use of these current concepts? This second question can no longer be decided scientifically; rather, in it both the limits of historical-scientific research and the incompetency of statements of faith in the sphere of science become apparent.

Only after these two critical preliminary questions are answered can one go on positively to determine what can be represented as Christology in a current theology of existence. Even here it is necessary to distinguish between two points of view:

First, the relation of existence and the Christ-myth is basically to be clarified; that is, the significance of existence for the understanding of the Christ-myth and vice versa the significance of the Christ-myth for the self-understanding of existence.

Second, it is to be especially observed how Jesus and, more especially the Apostle Paul actualized the Christ-myth and what these "actualizations" of Christ in history signify for our Christianity. —We begin with the historical, scientific problem of the relationship of the God-man of dogma to the eschatological Christ of the New Testament as this problem is posed for us by the current situation in New Testament research and in the history of dogma.

1. THE ESCHATOLOGICAL CHRIST AND THE GOD-MAN OF DOGMA

A new situation has been created in the discussion of the Christological problem by the so-called "thorough-going" eschatological method of regarding the New Testament proclamation and the dogmatic development of the first centuries. This "thorough-going" eschatology was introduced by Schweitzer and applied and tested by Martin

Werner in his book, *Entstehung des Christlichen Dogmas* (1941).* Before this time liberal theology had
stressed the human personality of the historical Jesus over
against the supernatural God-man of dogma, and therefore invited from the side of orthodoxy the not unjustified
charge that liberal theology falsified the Redeemer proclaimed in Scripture, in that it disrobed him of his di-
vinity and humanized him. Today, the representatives of
"thorough-going" eschatology are aware that the Christ,
as which Jesus expected to appear shortly for the judgment
of the world and as which the community formed by him
awaited him after his death, is no human, but a supernatural divine figure. But over against the representatives of
the dogma of the God-man, on the contrary, they referred
to this dogma as unscriptural, presenting a transformation
of the eschatological figure of Christ which was necessitated
by the delay of the expected return of Christ at the end-
time. Dependent upon the named scholars, we shall here
attempt to indicate several of the results of the "thorough-
going" eschatological method with reference to the relationship between the eschatological Christ and the God-
man of dogma, a problem upon which the historical-scientific discussion of the Christological question necessarily
concentrates.

Whatever one's confessional attitude toward Christ, *i.e.*
whatever concept of Christ may be determinative for faith,
one must concede nevertheless on purely historical and
scientific grounds that not only within the New Testament
different concepts of the Redeemer are present (Son of
David, Son of Man, Son of God, Gnostic Primeval Man,
Logos), but that above all a fundamental difference exists

*Translated by S. G. F. Brandon, as *The Formation of Christian Dogma:
An Historical Study of its Problem* (New York: Harper and Brothers,
1957).

between the eschatological concepts of the Messiah in the New Testament and the later ecclesiastical doctrine of the two natures in the Trinitarian Christological dogma. This substantial difference between the eschatological Christ and the God-man of dogma is evident as well in the form of the appearance of the Redeemer, as also especially in that which was ascribed to the primitive Christian eschatological Messiah and the God-man of dogma as redemptive work.

In the eschatological Christ we are dealing with a pre-existent angelic being who is elected and delegated by God for the inauguration of the new aeon in the end-time. The relationship of the man Jesus of Nazareth to this heavenly being is variously conceived. Either he was elevated after his death to a position of power, to which he knew himself called in his lifetime, or the heavenly being assumed form in him already on earth by transformation into an earthly person. In any case he will appear as the Son of Man in heavenly glory for the consummation of his saving work at the imminent end-time. There is no talk here of an encroachment on the deity of the Father by the deity of the Son, or of a putting in question of the divine nature of the Redeemer by his human nature—or vice versa, of his humanity by his deity, as when later the trinitarian and Christological controversies and the corresponding dogmas objectified his nature. As an angelic being the Messiah is a divine figure, but he is elected to his special position and this only for a definite period of time. His relation to the earthly person of Jesus of Nazareth is determined by the biblical concept of the possibility that angels transform themselves into human form, or that men can be elevated to God. A doctrine of the two natures in one person is therefore hardly necessary for this angel Christology.

The saving work of Christ moreover consists in the in-

auguration of the final, cosmic new aeon, through which
the reign of the demons is overcome and the Kingdom of
God is established as a new, perfect creation. If the par-
ticularities of this final drama, especially with regard to
the temporal realization of its individual acts, are partially
different in the New Testament, still the whole redeeming
work of the Messiah takes place within this framework.
Jesus understands his active works as well as passive experiences in this framework. As proclaimer of the imminent Kingdom and a corresponding behavior of those selected for it, he is the prophet. He goes to his death in
order to permit the last resistance of the demons to play
its full havoc and so through his suffering as a vicarious
sacrifice to remove the guilt standing in the way of the
coming of the Kingdom. In this death consists his high-
priestly work. As the one destined to become the Lord of
the future Kingdom he already now speaks and acts in full
regal authority, in that he bestows forgiveness and speaks
judgment, performs miracles, gathers the multitude of the
elect and appoints the judges of the Last Judgment.

What here still forms a unified eschatological whole has
become in the church dogma of the saving work of the
Redeemer—after it had endured painful embarrassment
and uncertainty for a long time with respect to it—a
Heilsgeschichte reaching over the centuries to a distant
future. Thereby it was assumed that some parts of that
original eschatological work of salvation were already fulfilled, while others were regarded as still belonging to the
future. In comparison with the final saving event assumed
in the New Testament to be already in progress, that
which is now regarded as already fulfilled represents only
a fragment—even then a completely altered one. The saving
work of Christ consists in this, namely, that he, through his

Incarnation and vicarious death, as well as by founding the Church as a sacramental institution of salvation, has created the possibility of redemption for men of all time. The extension of this saving work into a timeless-universal phenomenon cannot conceal the fact that we have to do here with a substitute for the eschatological expectation which was not fulfilled.

It is to the credit of Martin Werner's history of dogma that it showed how the sacramental work of salvation replaced the eschatological, and that this replacement occurred not only as a consequence of the transition of Christianity from Jewish territory to Hellenistic, but primarily in consequence of the recession of the primitive Christian expectation of the End, which was caused by the even longer delay of the Parousia. Above all, Werner demonstrated that this change in the conception of the work of redemption precipitated the change in the doctrine of the person of the Redeemer. As the basis of this new, non-eschatological doctrine of redemption, the eschatological Angel-Christ no longer sufficed, and had to be replaced— even if the mortal flesh would have to be deified through him—by the God-man, in whom this deification of the flesh first occurred and would again and again occur through the sacraments. The means for this transformation from the receding eschatological conception of redemption into a timelessly valid sacramental conception lay in Hellenism; this fact applies to both the work and the person of the Redeemer. The transformation occurred in such a way that it led to problems of the relation of the God-man Redeemer to God as Creator, and of the relation of the human and divine nature in the personality of the Redeemer. Such problems had not existed in the primitive Christian Angel-Christology. The further consequence was a long Trinitarian and Christological controversy which degenerated into the dogmatization of a God-man Redeemer, in which process the eschatological Christ is no longer recognized and to whom a totally different work of salvation is ascribed than had been experienced and expected in the faith of primitive Christianity.

As significant as this only quite briefly sketched view of dogmatic development appears in the light of "thoroughgoing" eschatology, it must be stressed that it is only a scientific reconstruction of history, an historical reconstruction which was conceived and can be maintained only by the greatest possible exclusion of a relation of the tradition to what we understand by existence. That which is its methodological, scientific advantage, if it is to be relevant for the theology of existence, must be experienced at the same time as imperfection and deficiency. For the theology of existence this total reconstruction to begin with is only of significance by virtue of the following factors: First, because as a scientific, historical construction it avoids being bound to some definite resultant stage of Christian dogma, in that it reveals to us the relativity of this formulation. On the other hand, it justifies on the grounds of the history of dogma our priority of soteriology over Christology by showing that Christology in its decisive periods of origin was determined by changes in soteriology. Even the further course of the history of dogma shows that Christology is not the presupposition of soteriology, but rather represents its mythological concretization. Christology as mythology is always Christology of existence and therefore in its significance is never to be conceived totally from scientific and historical perspectives. This judgment applies equally to the limits of the historico-scientific as well as to the *heilsgeschichtlich* understanding of Christology.

2. THE BOUNDARIES OF THE HISTORICO-SCIENTIFIC AND THE
"HEILSGESCHICHTLICH" UNDERSTANDING OF CHRISTOLOGY

For an historico-scientific method, as we have seen previously in the example of "thorough-going" eschatology,
the discussion of Christology is divided essentially into
three parts. First, it establishes the different mythological
and speculative-metaphysical conceptions in which Jesus
understood his own mission and in which the disciples of
Jesus afterwards sought to understand his person and work
as Redeemer. This messianic ideological material comprises the Old Testament and late Jewish concepts of the
Redeemer and its antecedents and parallels from the
history of religion, as well as the Gnostic-Hellenistic syn-
cretistic saviors, and extends through the history of theological and philosophical speculation down to the religious
hero, the teacher of wisdom, the Pietistic Savior and the
Christian principle of Neo-Protestant dogmatics. Second,
the science of history isolates the historical personality of
Jesus and seeks to establish with greatest objectivity—independently of how he has been understood and how we
today can understand his significance—the way in which he
understood himself in the context of his own time. Third,
and finally, historical research follows the changes which
the understanding of Jesus' appearance have undergone
from his own appearance at the beginning of our era
through all the epochs of the history of the Church and of
the humanity which came into touch with it down to the
present day, and strives to understand these changes in
their inner necessity as a whole. All three standpoints,
which are to be distinguished in research, but not to be
separated in practice, represent legitimate tasks and goals
of historico-scientific research in the Christological problem. But as necessary and fruitful as such historical indi-

vidual and total representations of Christology are, their limits should not be overlooked. The most competent and illuminating historico-scientific treatment of Christology, if it does not wish to deny its scientific character, will not overemphasize the value of a hypothetical construction which always needs correction and is always open to such. There is no absolute truth in science. Faith as absolute decision cannot appeal to it. Science cannot establish faith, but may preserve it from torpidity. On the other hand, we are dealing in Christology with statements of faith, that is, with that which cannot finally become an object of scientific research and presentation. If that happens anyway, and a scientific-historical judgment claims to be a statement about the worth and truth of Christology, then it can only err and become closed to that with which it really deals.

This judgment holds for all three directions of scientific research on Christology which were mentioned. If science pretends not only to explain the messianic myths, especially the eschatological Christ-myth, in their historical connections, but to make a judgment about their truth, then it can only speak of "primitive science" and irregular fantasy. It would thereby completely misunderstand the nature and significance of these phenomena, because, as expressions of the self-understanding of existence, they can only become vocal for existence. However, with such an attitude which is devoid of understanding science would only harvest the fruits of its own uncritical transgression of its boundary. The same must also be said if one thinks—in light of the thoroughly historically and scientifically grounded conclusion that Jesus was deceived in his expectation to appear to his contemporaries as the Son of Man on the clouds of heaven—he has said something about the significance of the appearance of Jesus other than that it cannot ultimately be conceived in scientific categories. Moreover, the same is true for the evaluation of the research methods and results of the history of dogma and theology. As instructive as is, for example, the view of the development of Christian dogma as the process of an advancing "de-eschatologizing" on the basis of the continued delay of the Parousia, it would err if it thought it could conceive in this way the authentic nature of these different forms of transformation of the Christian faith and its ideas of the Redeemer, and so to pass judgment on their value as truth. The self-understanding and the self-actualization of existence in relation to Transcendence with which it deals can never be fully grasped by means of a self-absolutizing historico-scientific hypothesis, however illuminating it may be in other respects. Existence is and remains the boundary of all scientific methods—as necessary as such scientific research, which is conscious of the limits of its capacity for knowledge, is for the faith of existence.

It is the advantage of the so-called *heilsgeschichtlich* understanding of Christology that it, for the sake of its faith-relationship to definite statements about events in history, is conscious of the limits of historical methods and is "aligned" with Christ and knows itself bound up with him in a history which remains ultimately inaccessible to scientific, historical categories. The danger of the *heilsgeschichtlich* theology, however, consists in the fact that it rejects, along with the history which transgresses its limits, the historico-scientific criticism which remains conscious of its competence and is indispensable for faith. Because of this, it accepts the mythology of *Heilsgeschichte* not as an expression of the self-understanding of existence, but as objective statements. In this way it becomes "superstitious" (*abergläubisch*) about mythology, in that it wishes to acknowledge the objectivity indispensable to the articulation of existence—that is, the corporeality of the myth as such—without reference to existence. It becomes uncritical with respect to the results of scientific-historical research, because it cannot listen to science due to the fact that science puts in question the validity of objective forms of mythology, for example, the spatio-temporality of the eschatological expectation. Thus it becomes finally intolerant with respect to its own historicality, in that it absolutizes to the universal validity of a dogma the unconditional attitude toward a definite tradition, which attitude is in itself appropriate to existence.

What we have here expressed about the limits of the scientific and the *heilsgeschichtlich* methods of Christology may at the same time be a contribution toward the clarification of the contemporary discussion of the problem of demythologizing. Beyond these critical considerations, the material which follows should point the way to a positive solution to this problem.

3. CHRIST-MYTH AND THE SELF-UNDERSTANDING OF EXISTENCE

The historico-scientific and the *heilsgeschichtlich* understanding of Christology at their limits point to the necessity of an understanding of Christology from the perspective of existence. For this existential dimension is lacking in the historico-scientific understanding and is demolished in the *heilsgeschichtlich* understanding by a misunderstanding of the nature of the myth. Myth is an expression of the self-understanding of existence. As the mythological image-world of existence is able to serve as an expression for the way in which existence understands itself, so vice versa can the transmitted mythology also be understood only from the perspective of existence.

From these general principles about the relationship of

myth and existence several important conclusions follow with respect to the relationship of the Christ-myth and existence.

It is not the task of a Christology of existence to create a new reconstruction beside the transmitted "picture" of Christ. Its task is rather to understand correctly the image of Christ in the tradition. The negative part of this task, namely, the refusal to produce a new Christ-myth, seems to contradict our statement that the myth is an expression of existential understanding. Why should a new myth not arise out of a new understanding of existence? Does not every generation possess its own myths? Why should our generation not beget its own Christ-myth? This point is not to be controverted in itself—especially not, since this production of myth is already going on today. But as is evident in the history of Christological reconstructions in recent times, this new begetting of myths is not advantageous. How pale, individual and abstract appears the divine teacher of wisdom, or the sentimental savior of Pietism, or the Christian principle over against the eschatological Christ, or even further, in comparison with the Gnostic speculations? Our thinking formed by scientific criticism is not conducive to the rise of myths. On such grounds the myth is always a product of uncritical self-absolutizing of a finite, objective perspective. The time of the origin of the great myths lies before the appearance of scientifically critical thinking. It must be said of the Christ-myth that it has become operative in definite acts of historicizing, above all, in connection with the historical appearance of Jesus of Nazareth and then in the form of acts of dogmatizing the Christ-figure. It follows as a consequence that a new Christ-myth is denied as a false Christ simultaneously by the representatives of an earlier Christ-myth, and that the representatives of a new Christ-myth must always ask themselves with what right they can appeal in their existential understanding to Christ, and whether their Christ-construction does not represent a break with rather than a transformation of the tradition. "What has Athens to do with Jerusalem?"—But even apart from our own historicality conditioned by science and Christian tradition, which does not contribute to the rise of a new Christ-myth, the moments of birth of an historically powerful myth are seldom. In the sea of mythological ideas and constructions there are only few really great Redeemer myths like that of the eschatological Christ. As archetypes they arise out of the unconscious, are formulated by prophets in outstanding hours of humanity and grow from generation to generation—until they become old and die.

In view of this genesis of myths in general and of the nature of the Christ-myth in particular, it would be comical if the theology of existence, for the sake of the significance which it attaches to the self-understanding of existence as the origin of myth, would come up with its own Christology. Theology is not prophecy, but just like the theology of existence, it is the interpretation of tradition. Even if the manner of its transforming appropriation of tradition is determinative for the future form of this tradition, it is itself, nevertheless, dependent upon the tradition. The Christ of the Christology of existence is therefore not a new Christ, that is, one beside the eschatological Christ to whom Jesus knows himself to be called, or the God-man of dogma, or the embodiment of the Christian principle, or the savior of the Pietists, etc. Standing in this tradition, it is rather the task of a Christology of existence to show that all these different representations of Christ are constructions, in that it recognizes in them the mythological expression of an experienced redemption—expressions which are only to be understood from a corresponding self-experience.

The recognition and validation of this correlation between the Christ-construction and existential experience form essential factors of the Christology of a theology of existence. From its general understanding of the relationship between myth and existence, it establishes not only this correlative relationship of representation and experience, but from this perspective it is further able positively to appreciate the different resultant stages of Christology, and so to attain, in the preservation of the special character of the different Christologies, a truly universal understanding of the different experiences of redemption expressed in them.

It is to be noticed first of all that the experiences of redemption underlying such Christological constructions stood also under the influence of a Christological construction, for otherwise they would not have been concretized again into a Christological construction. Even the experience of redemption, out of which the traditional Christologies are understood, must have arisen in a definite Christian tradition. This is proven by the fact that we do not have the same access to all transmitted Christological constructions, but rather some address us and disclose us to ourselves, while others remain strange and unintelligible to us.

This correlation, however, does not represent simply a static relationship. As the history of Christianity shows, there can always be new variations—whether it be that a traditional Christological formulation under definite conditions leads to a new understanding of existence which was not present in the tradition—or whether it be that from a new relation to existence it comes to a further formulation of traditional Christology in which the new understanding of existence arose.

In this way is indicated the manner in which Christological formulations arise and according to which these constructions have their history. Whatever is thereby objectively stamped in the formation of dogma, and whatever in dogmatic research can be conceived rationally and conceptually or intuitively in the course of subsequent experience—these are only the symbolic concretizations and their rational or biographical-psychical manifestations. The truth of the myth for existence, however, cannot be grasped in these objectified rational and psychical phenomena and with the categories corresponding to them. As every myth, so the Christ-myth discloses itself as truth only to the faith of existence living in it, a faith which as such cannot be objectified, but before, after and in all conceptual illumination is absolute decision. The so-called messianic self-consciousness of Jesus, the Pauline "In-Christ" formula, Lutheran theologizing of the cross or even a Redeemer-Pietism, may be analyzed and explained religio-historically or religio-psychologically—but nothing is thereby said about the truth of this understanding of Christ for the believer, as little as any such mythological expression for the self-understanding of existence may be justified or confuted in this manner. By the manner in which it believes, existence decides for itself in each case to what extent a myth is true for it.

This curtailment of the possibility of a universally valid statement about the truth of the understanding of Christ presupposed by existence provides, nevertheless, an objective criterion for the appropriateness of a Christology. This criterion grows out of the recognition of the function which Christology—according to its nature—has within theology. Christology as part of the doctrine of redemption is concerned with the exposition of the creative activity of God through which man in suffering and guilt participates in redemption. For the theology of existence this means that Christology is the mythical expression of the self-understanding of existence in which existence in relation to Transcendence experiences itself in its freedom as a gift. Christology fulfils this essential function to the extent that in it—over against self-redemption, but also over against every exclusion of man—the character of existence as grace is expressed. Attention is thereby focused upon the formative power which such a Christology exercises upon existence which understands itself in it and finally, beyond the historical power, to the capacities of human existence which are disclosed through it.

Just from these perspectives of the pure grace-like character of existence, the formative power for existence, and the capacities of existence, there result the varying degrees of appropriateness and value among the Christological possibilities of expression, granted that their differences are recognized. From these aspects, as will be shown in conclusion, the eschatological Christology in which Jesus and the primitive Church lived proves to be of special significance for the Christology of existence.

4. JESUS THE CHRIST

Jesus is the Christ—in this formula the Christology of primitive Christianity, which coincides with Jesus' messianic claim, can be comprehended. As for Jesus messianology, so for primitive Christianity Christology is no mere mythology, but a mythology historicized in existential understanding. Dogmatically objectified, it represents an error, but this judgment does not apply to the truth of faith which is expressed in it. Such a judgment is incorrect only when it is objectified. Apart from such a criticism it is not acceptable to us. Faith does not mean to repeat statements which are objectively false.

Jesus is the Christ—that cannot mean for us that we regard him, on the basis of his promises and correspondingly the expectations of his community, to be the Messiah who will come soon on the clouds of heaven to execute the Last Judgment. Rather: for the theology of existence as grace, it becomes meaningful for us by showing how Jesus understood himself and was understood by the community as the Christ. The historical formative power which this faith of Jesus and his disciples possesses, and the capacities of human existence which appear in it are just those elements which give this figure a special revelatory quality for us. Not in historical or dogmatic objectivity can we repeat the confession of the primitive Church—"Jesus is the Christ"; rather, we are able to recognize in it the revelation of God as the Redeemer and it becomes for us in this manner the legitimate mythological symbol for existence as grace.

The incarnate God of the Trinitarian Christological dogma, or the figure of the savior which encounters the believer, or even the divine teacher of eternal truths can well be understood as an expression of the fact that existence is grace. For in the God-man Christology it is God who becomes man—real man, *vere homo, vere Deus*. Redemption is through God, but in human form. Even so in the religiosity of Pietism the savior is encountered whose gift is salvation. But in this pietistic devotion everything depends on the fact that salvation is really experienced and does not remain simply a divine promise. And finally, two things are true also of the timelessly valid, absolute truth of Christianity: this truth is eternally divine and nevertheless discovered by man.

Even if interpreted as expressions of the self-understanding of existence, however, these types of Christology
are scarcely to be compared with the myth of the eschatological Christ and the way in which Jesus understood himself
and was understood by the disciples. What is the significance of all Trinitarian Christological speculations, all
experiences with the Savior, all speculations about the relation of the finite spirit to the Absolute Spirit, in comparison with the myth of the in-break of a perfect, new
creation through the appearance of the Messiah and the
way in which Jesus and the apostles understood and actualized their existence in this mythology? Here salvation is
really the total creation of God, completely out of human
hands, and yet man understands himself as the creature
destined to a new Being, and he is summoned to the realization of the same freedom and responsibility. The actualization of eschatology in imminent expectation and
contemporary event in Jesus and the Apostle Paul represents an expression of the consciousness of existence as
grace which is hardly to be surpassed, and is as well a powerful symbol of such an understanding of existence.

In this way we stand firm by the second peculiarity of
mythology actualized by Jesus' messianic consciousness and
acts, and by the eschatological Christ-mysticism of the
Apostle Paul: namely, the intensity and historical formative power of its existential understanding.

The theology of the Trinitarian Christological dogma
certainly knows not only of a saving act within God Himself, but also of *opera ad extra* and their enactment as well as
of the possibility of a *unio mystica* of the justified with God,
and finally of a *visio beatifica* beyond. Pietistic belief in
the savior certainly knows of a mystical experience. The
speculations about the spirit see indeed in everything
finite the divine germinal substance waiting to be released.

But how supraworldly, how merely internal and how abstractly unreal these constructions are over against the eschatological activity of Jesus and the eschatological existence of the Pauline "life in Christ!"

How this-worldly, soberly and concretely Jesus' consciousness of election expresses itself over against these concepts! He expects the Kingdom of God for this world. But he does not delude himself about the demonic powers which oppose its realization. He is by no means merely the one who waits patiently, but actively in the sacrifice of his life shows to his own disciples how for them in need and sin there are possibilities for real victory. Similarly, the Apostle Paul is not content with a merely fictitious, or only future victory, but in the community of dying and rising with Christ he understands his life as a new Being in which he participates.

Still much less possible for us as an illustration of the intensity and formative power of this eschatological Christ is here a description of the attitudes toward values of human existence which emerge in connection with this phenomenon in history and remain active in successive generations, or are ever awakened anew. Whatever in the way of ethical values or manifestations have emerged in the course of history, these—though with manifold transformations—go back essentially to the way in which Jesus understood himself as the Christ and was understood as such by others.

There must be an enormous depth and inexhaustible fulness of possibilities of understanding and realization of human life in the eschatological Christology of the New Testament which stands over against us, that through all the changes, additions, deviations and distortions it has been understood continually by men as the revelation of the redeeming grace of God, and has occasioned the confession that here God became man, and the temporal turning point of history had taken place.

On theological, existential and ethical grounds Christ Jesus is of immense significance for a Christology of existence. In that—according to the primitive Christian testimony—the Christ-myth became historical in and through him, he represents the prototype of a Christology of existence. Therefore, the Christology of existence conceives its task to be to transfer Jesus Christ from the historical past into the historicality of the contemporary existence by means of the transforming appropriation of the self-understanding of existence, and to permit that history and its own historicality to fulfil themselves as *Heilsgeschichte*.

This task, however, goes beyond the structuring of a Christology of existence as is here attempted and points to the nature of the last chapter of this dogmatic compendium which will be dedicated to the questions of the appropriation of salvation and of fulfilment.

CHAPTER 5

CHRISTIAN EXISTENCE
IN TIME

In connection with Christology and Soteriology as the doctrines of the basic possibility and realization of salvation, it is customary in dogmatics to speak more especially of the concrete mediations and realizations of redemption in history, and, at the same time, to regard them in terms of the consummation in eternity, a consummation which points beyond time and history. This matter is treated in the doctrinal subdivisions of means of salvation, Church and Last Things. All three sections deal, though each in a special way, with visible manifestations of Christian existence in time. Salvation attained through Christ is appropriated by the believer through the Word and sacraments. Therefore they are called "means of salvation." The Church not only avails itself of these means of salvation intrusted to it, but also represents the sphere of history stamped by them. It is therefore defined as the *communio sanctorum,* which is to be understood partly as communion with the Holy One and partly as community of the saints. According to the doctrine of the Church, neither individual existence nor the existence of the Church is consummated in time. The life of the individual continues after death in the beyond, and, together with the world in which the Church has her history, it will find its fulfilment at the Last Judgment. Although the Last Things signify the overcoming of space and time, they are nevertheless represented as spatio-temporal events.

Theology of existence is interested in these doctrines not only because it is present in the tradition and arose in tension with it, but because here we are dealing with that which forms the intention of these dogmatic *loci,* namely, with the concrete realization of existence in history. Theology of existence is concerned also with the manner of the mediation of the tradition and its contents for existence, the community which belongs to existence, and the end and fulfilment of history, in which existence stands alone and in community.

The Christian doctrinal tradition here being examined has produced a series of contradictory conceptions and unsolved problems in each of the three main sections mentioned above. We call attention here merely to the most crucial of these difficulties in which the Christian confessions and epochs have been chiefly divided.

In consequence of the Reformation we customarily include among the means of salvation the word of Scripture in the proclamation of the Church, as well as the sacraments of Baptism and the Lord's Supper. Contrary to this list, the Catholic Church recognizes seven sacraments, and these form for it the authentic means of salvation. The difference appears most acutely in a comparison of the Catholic Mass with the Protestant worship service. From their understanding of justification through faith alone apart from works of law, the Reformers regarded as unscriptural magic the sacramental mediation of grace which enables one to perform meritorious works. However, measured by Scripture, the doctrines of Baptism and the Lord's Supper as expressed by the Reformers are no less problematic, as is evident from the controversies over these points in the time of the Reformation. In view of the spiritualizing of the concept of grace by the Reformers, it must be regarded as problematic to what extent one can still speak here of sacraments as distinguished from the activity of the Word. Already in the Reformation two lines are marked off. On the one side, the Word is understood sacramentally, while on the other the sacrament is seen as merely a symbol. The sacramental understanding of the Word leads subsequently to the assertion of the activity of the Word *extra usum*; the symbolic conception leads on the contrary to a rationalism which empties the symbol so that it becomes a mere sign. In any case, the relation of word and sacrament poses a problem for Protestantism.

Connected with this problem is the problematic character of the concept of the Church. For Roman Catholicism, the Church is a sacramental institution of salvation, founded by Christ and hierarchically organized. As a natural-supernatural phenomenon it spans time and eternity. The Reformers correctly recognized that through the centuries a hierarchy and sacramentalism had been constructed which cannot be grounded on Scripture. But even though they thought that they were able to solve the problem of the relation of the one true Church to the different manifestations of the Church in time by distinguishing between the invisible and visible Church, this solution is not only unscriptural, but also practically unsatisfying. Instead of *one* Church which asserts that it was founded by Christ to be alone the true Church, now there are a multitude of different churches all claiming to be the visible embodiment and chosen instrument of the one invisible Church. Neo-Protestantism with its secularization of the Church into a this-worldly cultural phenomenon curbed the controversy of the confessions and in its own way reflected something of the universal expectation of primitive Christianity. But the fate of this culture-faith and the science of the New Testament have given us the insight that it is not possible to group Church, culture and Kingdom of God so neatly under one common denominator.

Thus the discussion of the question of the Church leads to the problem of eschatology. While the Reformation, with the exception of the cancellation of the doctrine of purgatory, deviated only in unessential points from the traditional conception of Last Things, it was Neo-Protestantism which here brought the great transformation. This change in respect to the doctrine of Last Things, as already indicated, took place in two phases in such a way that these two stages of reorientation stand in exclusive opposition to one another. In the eighteenth and the beginning of the nineteenth century, the culture-optimism of Neo-Protestantism led to a spiritualizing, if not to say dissolution, of the traditional eschatology of the Church, both in its individual and in its universal dimensions. The prospect of the immortality of the soul located in the this-worldly reality and a continued development of history actualizing the victory of spirit over nature formed the crowning conclusion of these dogmatic systems. At the end of the nineteenth and the beginning of the twentieth century the illusory character of that eschatological culture-optimism, as well as the quite different meaning of primitive Christian eschatology, was recognized in the progress of research and under the impression of temporal experiences of just this Neo-Protestantism. For primitive Christianity, eschatology was not merely a more or less harmless closing chapter of dogmatics; rather, its message is basically and totally eschatological, in that all its statements proceed from the presupposition of the end-event which is imminent or already in progress. Primitive Christian existence is eschatological existence. It is quite different from immortality of the soul in a region beyond and from cultural development always climbing higher—but at the same time also different from the latest attempts of Protestant theology to transform this primitive Christian eschatological existence again into an objective otherworldly and *heilsgeschichtlich* theology.

If therefore statements about means of salvation, Church and Last Things as forms of Christian existence in time will be made here by the theology of existence, this can only happen by examining first the origin of the obviously problematic character of the corresponding points of Christian doctrine.

1. MYTHOLOGICAL OBJECTIVATION AND THE REALIZATION OF EXISTENCE

All the different conceptions of means of salvation, Church and Last Things which have arisen in the course of history appeal or go back to the relevant statements in the New Testament. For Catholicism and Old Protestantism, these are valid as a normative source of revelation, for Neo-Protestantism at least as historical documents of its own heritage. In order to understand the disagreement of the doctrinal formulations and historical types which have arisen on this basis, to which we have called attention by way of introduction, it is necessary to bear in mind the difference and at the same time the connection between mythological objectivation and realization of existence. Under this aspect, which results from our concept of existence, an objective estimation of the different types, as well as a conquest of their problematic character seems to us possible.

What encounters us in the New Testament as the

preaching of the Word of God, as sacramental mediation of salvation in Baptism and the Lord's Supper, as community of the elect believers, as description of the anticipated bliss and as conduct in the beginning of the end-time—these are mythological objectivations which serve as expressions and forms of appearance of the self-understanding and realization of existence. The mythological character of these concepts and constructions becomes immediately clear when we try to conceive them in a scientifically objective manner. We can establish in this way that here men appeared with the claim to be preaching God's Word rather than a human word, and that faith was given to them as a gift, or that here sacramental acts were performed, Baptism and Eucharist, through which a divine supernatural salvation was mediated to the participants. Or further it might be established that here communities are formed which live from this faith, that they belong to the multitude of those elected to be participants in the Kingdom of God or the body of Christ. Statements are made dealing with the course of final events, with the nearness of the "in-breaking" or with individual events which have already occurred and that which is still expected. The result is that the believers conduct themselves accordingly, no longer reckon with a lengthy duration of this world and know themselves already to be a new creature which death cannot harm.

Although these testimonies and phenomena have a spatio-temporal character, emerge in time and space, and operate in conjunction with time and space, at the same time they transcend the context of space and time, allow the eternal to break into time, so that the finite becomes for them transparent for the other-worldly. The reality of what is meant and represented in the mythologically objective statements and formulations is not accessible to scientific thinking which operates within the categories of space and time. A space in which the laws of space no longer hold, a time in which time is overcome, an existence which is no longer finite, a history which is no longer earthly—these are impossibilities for conceptual-theoretical thinking. If it does not wish to abandon itself, it can speak here only of presumption and delusion.

Such a judgment upon the New Testament ideas and uses of the word of God and the sacraments, of the Church and the Body of Christ, and finally, of eschatology seems to be unavoidable. That a word is not a human, but a divine word cannot be demonstrated; rather, there is present in the New Testament the temporal historical conditionality of that which is here understood as the word of God. The entire situation proclaimed here as God's saving decree proves to be an illusion when compared with the actual course of history. Therefore the sacraments cannot have the force ascribed to them, that is, to mediate to those for whom they are performed, or who take part in them, the reality of the new Aeon. On the same grounds, moreover, the Ecclesia cannot be the community of those elected to participate in the final kingdom, or of those who have already participated in its new corporeality.

All these mythological objectivations prove to be untenable in history, and were soon exposed, already within the New Testament, to the most radical transformations. As these transformations of primitive Christianity are transformations of earlier objectivations which were eschatological, formed the community and expressed the means of salvation; so they in the further course of history were transformed and newly employed according to the ideas and thoughts of other times. Just in these considerations consists the nature and function of mythological objectivation, that in *it* a formative and substantial force appears in history, and that this force, instead of being able to take refuge in this formulation, is itself subject to the same constant transformation. The history of the Christian means of salvation, the Church and its eschatology affords rich illustrative material for this fact.

To understand this history in its different and opposing resultant formulations from its origin to the present, another factor must certainly be considered. Up to now we have spoken of the means of salvation, the Church and Last Things only as mythological objectivations, how they are conceivable by conceptual-objective thinking and by it have been transformed in accord with its consciousness of reality and employed in each new situation. But then mythological objectivation means objectivation of something which is by nature not an object, but is merely objectified. Even in the consciousness of reality in conceptual-objective thinking we are not dealing merely with something which can be adequately grasped in this manner; it rather pertains to that sphere which is only illumined by this thinking, but cannot be encompassed. This reality which is objectified in myth and only to be illumined by theoretical thinking is the reality of existence; that is, of that authentic existence which knows itself related in faith to Transcendence and is experienced in its realization as grace.

In the eschatological mythology of primitive Christianity and the conceptual-objective thinking standing in its tradition we are dealing with this reality of the self-understanding and realization of existence inaccessible to conceptual-objective knowledge. Existence is that which knows itself to be addressed in the human word by God's word. Existence is that by which salvation is mediated through the sacrament. Existence is that which can experience itself bound up with other existence in a no longer world-

ly community. For existence, finiteness becomes transparent to eternity, and existence experiences history as
Heilsgeschichte. For existence, eschatology is the expression of its self-understanding.

To the extent that existence actualizes itself in the concepts and behavioral patterns of such mythological objectivations, it becomes conscious in thinking self-illumination
of the difference between its actualization as existence and
the mythological objectivations as forms of expression and
manifestations of that actualization. Without this distinction, which is only possible by means of conceptual thinking, it would become a victim to fantasy and delusion.
With this distinction, we stand at the other and authentic
origin of the history of Christian means of salvation, Church
and eschatology—an orgin which is material rather than
formal. These constructions, in their origin and in their
history, are authentic reality only for the one who, as believing existence, is actualized in them and receives himself as a gift. Therefore, as every scientific presentation of
the theology of the New Testament and of the history of
dogma shows, they continually assume new forms and
continually receive other contents. Otherwise than in creative appropriation, existence, which stands in tradition,
cannot be actualized. The Apostle Paul explained in this
respect—just because he understood his existence in Christ
—that he knows Christ no longer after the flesh, but only
the Christ after the Spirit (2 Cor. 5:16). Therefore, the
revelation in which he participates is a special revelation,
as he continually stressed as evidence that he stood within
the tradition. The sacraments, therefore, have a special
significance for him, a significance which corresponds to
his situation. There is therefore a Pauline concept of the
Church as the Body of Christ and a Pauline pattern of the
final end of history. These concepts represent neither

merely historical curiosities nor *the* Church nor *the* Last Things, but are truth for the faith of Paul and for the one who stands with him in the genuine community of existence.

Instead of pursuing further the perspective of a critical and positive understanding of the historical characteristics of the means of salvation, the Church and Last Things which we have inaugurated, we wish rather to develop, on the basis of the stated definition of the relationship of mythological objectivation and actualization of existence, the implications of a theology of existence as means of salvation, Church and eschatology. There the opportunity presents itself to return to some typical formulations of these doctrines which have arisen in history.

2.   WORD AND SACRAMENT AS SYMBOLS
FOR EXISTENCE

If we here consider word and sacrament as means of salvation for existence, so we affirm already with this choice that we stand with our understanding of the means of salvation on the groundwork of the Reformation and therefore in opposition to the Catholic conception. This is not our choice, but has been decided in the tradition in which we stand and which we have not selected ourselves. For a theology of existence as is framed here, the means of salvation are not at all the Catholic sevenfold sacraments, but the word of Scripture and the sacraments of Baptism and the Lord's Supper. Nothing is thereby said against the possibility that the seven sacraments of the Catholic Church can also be means of salvation. Against all the Reformation devaluation of these seven sacraments as unscriptural magic, history and the present attest rather that now and then they have worked as means of salvation and are still working. That they do not have this force for the one standing outside this tradition does not speak against their truth, but is rather a proof for the limited number of possibilities of understanding necessarily bound up with each historical tradition.

That is certainly not a judgment in the sense of Reformation theology, for this theology did not know the distinction between mythological objectivation and actualization of existence which leads the theology of existence to take such a position. Between the Reformation and the theology of existence stands the irreversible development of Neo-Protestantism. For this Neo-Protestantism, the Reformation use of the Word of God as a means of salvation is in many respects no less mythological and magical than the Roman sacramentalism. But now the theology of existence does not enable us to be unfair toward the Reformation understanding of the means of salvation. On the contrary, from the perspective of existence the new understanding of means of salvation with which the Reformation concerned itself appears as an attempt to abandon a mechanical, superstitious use of the means of salvation without thereby falling into a rationalistic emptying of the mythical symbols. This is the basic problem in the controversy between Luther and Zwingli over the Lord's Supper. Zwingli struggled with brilliant understanding against superstition, and Luther opposed him out of the traditional historicality of his existence, to which belonged as well what seems to us as mythology and magic. The theology of existence takes into account the intentions of both, understanding word and sacrament as symbols for existence.

In so far as the theology of existence—as the conceptual illumination of the faith—is a science, but is at the same time an expression of a faith and an appeal to existence which are no longer scientifically conceivable, the Word has for it a two-fold significance and function. As a means for the scientific, conceptual illumination of faith, of its tradition and the understanding thereof, of its self-actualization and forms of expression, the Word is for it a sign with whose help an unequivocal description of the content of consciousness and logical operations are possible. These conceptual signs are, as a rule, drawn from the tradition, but their significance and association occur with consent and can therefore also be altered. Conceptual language is the creation and tool of the understanding.

For existence "word" is quite another matter. For the thinking of existence the word is also primarily a conceptual sign. Without the aid of conceptual thinking no knowledge or communication of knowledge is possible, and as well, no knowledge of existence and no statements about existence. But existence, which is experienced as grace in the actualization of its relation to Transcendence, can no longer be conceptually objectified. Neither authentic existence nor personal failure, neither Transcendence nor grace can as such be objectified. If it happens nevertheless—and it happens whenever we wish to speak of them in any other way—then these objectivations are no longer conceptual signs which can be used with consent in theoretical thinking; rather, in them we have to do with symbols for existence. The word, which for the understanding represents a conceptual sign, becomes for existence a symbol of possible self-understanding and possible self-actualization. The symbol is also an objectivation, but not from and for understanding, but rather from and for existence. As the symbol arising from existence represents an expression of the self-understanding of existence, so it appears again in the self-understanding of existence and is interpreted by existence in a transforming appropriation. On this basis the symbol is neither arbitrary nor abstract, but historically concrete. It is, as it were, the incarnation of existence.

Therefore the myth even more than metaphysical speculation is well suited to serve as a linguistic symbol of existence. However, no manner of speaking is excluded from playing the role of a symbol for existence.

Where it happens that a word becomes an incarnate symbol for existence, there it has become a medium of salvation. In this sense the Word of Scripture is used in the proclamation of the Church, in preaching as well as in the "care of souls." Proclamation is not simply the recitation of the record of the mythological data of the biblical *Heilsgeschichte* and the assertion of the reality of the events narrated in it, nor is it concerned with deriving from it universally valid truths in the sense of results of science and then discussing them. The proclamation of the word as a means of salvation rather employs conceptual-objective thinking and speaking in order to allow the mythological symbols to become vocal for existence as symbols of the self-understanding of existence. The mythological expression for the success of the understanding is the testimony of the Holy Spirit. Therefore, proclamation occurs under the invocation of the Holy Spirit who is for existence neither magical nor rational, but is the actualization of the mythical symbol in a concrete historical situation.

The same is true as well for the other kinds of means of salvation, namely, the sacraments. For existence, no other significance and function can be ascribed to the sacraments than those which the word already possesses for existence. The sacraments can be symbols of the self-understanding of existence only in a form in which they become for the existence of others the occasion and possibility of an analogous self-actualization in an interpretative appropriation of its content. Since with regard to the word this form is not a mere replaceable sign, but is historically concrete; so in place of the word a definite, his-

torically stamped action can also appear. Because these
sacramental acts can be understood by existence only as
symbols, every magical misuse is excluded at the outset.
On the other hand, the proclamation of the word through
its connection with the sacraments is also preserved from
the danger of intellectualistic misunderstanding which
otherwise threatens. While the word can be understood and
employed by itself alone as a mere conceptual sign, such
an understanding and use is excluded when the word
stands in connection with the sacrament. For the activity
of the sacrament can be misinterpreted magically, but not
rationally as a mere sign, because it represents something
which is not merely conceptual.

On this basis, theology of existence acknowledges the
fact that for it in the Christian tradition, not merely the
word alone, but sacraments are transmitted in connection
with it as means of salvation, and it will employ them in
the sense already mentioned. Since it has the development
of Christian dogma in Protestantism as a presupposition, it
will thus confine itself to the use of Baptism and the Lord's
Supper. As little as in respect to the traditional Christologies, does it know itself here summoned to a restoring re-
sumption of the forms which have become strange to it,
and to a critical withdrawal from the forms of its tradition which are still vital. It sees its task rather as pointing
the way and remaining open to an interpretation and use
of the sacraments of Baptism and the Lord's Supper as
means of salvation for existence.

In this sense theology of existence understands Baptism
as a symbol of that reality which is meant for existence
with the concepts of creation and providence, sin and redemption. The symbol is valid for those who participate
in the act to the degree that they are enabled to transform
the outer activity of the sacrament into an inner activity

of the self-realization of existence in community. Such can happen both in the enactment of the sacrament and in later appeal to it; but in every instance where it happens, it is a becoming aware—and as such an operation—of the redeeming grace of God.

In the Lord's Supper this grace-like existence is symbolized by the common partaking of the bread and wine, in remembrance of that celebration which Jesus had with his disciples before his death, in which he, according to the tradition, mediated to them in this form participation in salvation. As little as the proclamation of the Church can be grounded upon the historical missionary command, or Baptism upon the so-called "command to baptize"— even so little can the practice of the Lord's Supper be justified as historically founded by Jesus. Within the time foreseen in the early Christian eschatological means of salvation, a means of salvation exhibits its legitimacy only by the fact that it is a real means of salvation. Thus the sacrament of the Lord's Supper fulfils its determination for existence if the suffering and death of Jesus and the meanings which are bound up with it in his community become operative in such a way that existence in community is experienced as grace.

It should not be necessary, but—in view of occasional misunderstandings and a reversed practice corresponding to them—it is not superfluous to remark that the means of salvation, the sacraments no less than the Word, may not be confined to cultic use and practice in the Church. As the meaning of the proclaimed word is not exhausted when an event of salvation is merely proclaimed, but rather when this event of salvation actualizes itself in the self-understanding of existence; so the sacrament is not fulfilled in the enactment of the sacramental activity as such. Rather, this must be translated and so continued in an inner activity of those who participate in the sacrament. But even in this inner activity the means of salvation do not attain their goal. This enactment within represents only a threshold of their redeeming activity; for from the inner experience they demand to become operative again in the outwardly visible existence, in the behavior of the individual and the formation of the community. Only in this formative power for human life and corporate life do they find their fulfilment—so far as one can speak of fulfilment in history as such. The means of salvation are by nature not content with a mythological incarnation in symbolic speech and action, but wish—from the perspective of the self-understanding occasioned by them and by means of the self-actualization of existence produced by them—to transform the individual and corporate life of man in accord with their meaning.

This sphere of the use of Christian means of salvation and their operation as a transforming power in life and history forms the content of the Christian Church, of the *communio sanctorum* which as communion with the Holy One should be at the same time the community of the saints. In view of the different formulations making the claim for this distinction and of the manifoldness of their normative definitions, the question of the nature and the truth of the Church is posed for us.

3. THE CHURCH AS CHRISTIAN EXISTENCE IN COMMUNITY

Seen historically, all phenomena in history in which in one way or another Christian means of salvation are employed and are active in forming community, will have to be regarded as the Christian Church. The Christian Church is the sphere of the use and active operation of the Christian means of salvation. The Christian character of the means of salvation here put in question follows—historically regarded—from the fact that they stand in some kind of positive relation to the appearance, preaching and activity of Jesus of Nazareth and the history of Christianity proceeding from them. Regarded purely historically, the designation "Christian" cannot be denied to any of the sociological phenomena arising in this connection—so long as they make this claim. A denial of the Christian character of such a church and an elevation of one special type to *the Church* is in this context all the less possible since the heterogeneity and contrariety, the exclusivity of its claims for validity and the mutual anathematizing of these formulations which have characterized their history, retreat behind the commonality of their mutual opposition. They are all bound together in the commonality, and in the mutual opposition they are all actually found in respect to their historical origin—whether they wish to admit it or not.

The early Christian Ecclesia does not represent a phenomenon to whose nature belongs a development in history or which can appear at just any arbitrary point of time, as is the case with these formations; rather, the primitive Christian Ecclesia is for Jesus the multitude of those elected by community with him to participate in the coming Kingdom of God. For the Apostle Paul it represents as the Body of Christ that realm in which the new form of the world has already become a reality under the guise of the disappearing of the old Aeon. The primitive Christian Church, as primitive Christian existence, is an eschatological phenomenon. From the perspective of the method of "thorough-going eschatology," the history of the Christian Church exhibits itself in its entire heterogeneity and contrariety as the totality of the necessarily different attempts to transform the originally eschatological conception of the Church into the course of history determined by the delay

of the End, and to develop it. Out of this historical necessity determinative for the first collecting of the eschatological community by Jesus, the original community characterized by faith in the inbreaking "turning point of
time" was changed into the catholic Church as an institution of salvation encompassing the world and the world
beyond. A further stage of this process of "de-eschatologizing" is the visible Church of the Reformation which is conscious of itself as the embodiment of the true invisible
Church. From this Church of the Reformation came finally the cultural character of the Neo-Protestant concept
of the Church, in which the supernatural event of salvation was changed into a process of cultural development
within the world.

From this perspective in which all other sociological
phenomena of Christian faith which have appeared in the
course of time may be arranged, there results for the theology of existence in turn the necessity to ground the concept of the Church, not dogmatically and historically upon
an illusory *Heilsgeschichte* or a hypostatized history, but
upon the self-understanding of existence in community. At
the same time, however, the possibility also exists for it to
refute every position which questions the concept of the
Church based upon the self-understanding of existence as
being itself a historically demonstrable self-misunderstand-
ing. In this we must certainly be conscious that the problem
of the Church in its depths can neither be grasped nor
solved on the scientifico-historical level, but represents a
question of self-understanding. Therefore, after these in-
dications of the historical state of the problem, we turn
in what follows to a discussion of the concept of the Church
from the perspective of existence.

What the Church can be for the theology of existence
ensues directly from the nature of existence. In its authen-

tic existence (*Selbstsein*) as grace related to Transcendence, existence (*Existenz*) knows that it is never alone, neither as regards its origin in the past nor its existence in the present and future. As a phenomenon standing within tradition, it expresses itself as determined by that heritage which it meets and adopts in its historical situation. Self-actualization in an appropriating transformation of the tradition is its present. In that it is what it is in time, it simultaneously becomes determinative for the future. What it understands and how it is itself understood belong no less to existence than how it understands itself. It possesses its truth not for itself, but only in community. Existence is in the truth only in community. Truth for it is no finished product, but the current unconditionality of authentic existence in community. What of it appears in space and time as individual form and community formations is not the truth of existence itself, but its objectivation in the contemporary historical situation. As unconditioned as these formulations are for existence, even so they do not raise the claim to absoluteness, but rather remain open for rational illumination, and can ultimately be understood only by existence with which they want to stand in community within and beyond all organization. The differences and diversities which emerge in such encounters with existence form the cause of arguments and divisions; but for existence it is just that which is alien to it which is the occasion for always renewed re-examination of one's own position rather than anxious self-assertion and self-assured condemnation of what is different. Lack of understanding and of being understood always reminds existence of the imperfection of its truth and causes it to seek new ways of attaining community.

The gist of this line of argument is that Christian existence and Christian existence in community cannot be something basically different from existence and existence in community. Christian existence is determined by the fact that it is existence which stands within the Christian tradition, and Christian existence in community is existence which is realized in a definite Christian way in community with the existence of others. In the fact that the Christian tradition in the course of its history, as we have indicated by reference to the process of de-eschatologizing as its formative principle, has assumed so many different forms exclusive of one another—in this fact lies the reason that the Christian understanding of existence necessarily had to assume different forms and will continue to do so. We can therefore by no means speak of one true Church which is generally demonstrable. None of the different churches arising out of the special tradition of their historical situation can correctly make the claim of absolute validity for its form. This is true not merely on the basis of the insight into the general relativity of historical phenomena, or of the insight into the special problem which for the Christian Church is connected with the non-fulfilment of the eschatological expectation of the Kingdom of God, but rather on the positive basis that existence can be actualized only in its historicality unconditionally, but not with universal validity. It is a consequence of the perspective of existence that the one true Church can only be believed.

In this nature of existence lies the possibility for overcoming the relativism bound up necessarily with every merely historical method, and for the realization of a community, as would be impossible by the absolutizing of an historical phenomenon. As existence in each of these instances, so existence standing in any Christian tradition can realize community with respect both to the past and the future only by taking seriously the unchangeable historical situation of its present. This situation is for it anything but arbitrary. Existence can as little choose its present as its past. As it can only take over the latter, so can the former only be actualized through it. The criticism or rejection of a heritage of the historical past represents nevertheless an after-effect of that heritage—just as not only that with which existence feels itself related, but also its opposite belongs to its self-realization. In this way the future is already determined, for it will not take place apart from what is present for existence. For existence, nevertheless, everything is not a coercive course, as it is for theoretical thinking; rather, existence chooses in unconditionality and in this way actualizes itself.

Thus in the course of history the Christian churches appear as the historical manifestations of the actualization of existence in community. But for every realization of existence in community, every absolutizing of itself as a universally valid provable manifestation of *the* Christian Church is a betrayal of its truth. Therefore, the Church as Christian existence in community remains in its consciousness of its unconditionality open for the possibility of an existence of the Church which is not its possibility— without slipping into relativism. And therefore the genuine Church possesses its Fathers and its confessions, as it speaks also of heretics and heresy. But in its historicality heretics and heresy belong to it no less than its Fathers and confessions. By remaining open in unconditionality it exhibits its true catholicity which is basically different from dogmatic absolutism, but is not to be confused with a universalism which relativizes everything. Only on this basis are possible a tolerance, which does not lead to self-negation, and a mission, which does not mean violation of the one who believes differently. These are necessary as evidence of the fact that the Christian Church knows of its unconditionality in historicality, in which it is actualized as the true temporal community of existence.

With such an understanding of the historical appearance of the Church, the theology of existence believes it is able to take into account the early Christian formation of community, as well as the formulations which have arisen in the course of history, such as the Catholic natural-supernatural institution of salvation, the Reformation concept of the visible form of the invisible Church and the Neo-Protestant transformation of the Kingdom of God into a cultural phenomenon on earth—and to preserve itself from such misunderstanding. It belongs to its task also to reckon with the other components of these conceptions which hitherto have not been positively considered: the concepts of the other world and ideas of immortality, the doctrines of the Last Judgment and of eternal fulfilment. What role do these mythologies and speculations, with which the traditional concepts of the Church are connected in various ways, play in a theology of existence?

4. "THE WORLD BEYOND" AND "HEILSGESCHICHTE" OF EXISTENCE

The primitive Christian Church lived in the expectation of the coming Kingdom and believed itself to be selected to participate in it. As the Body of Christ it represented that realm in which the final event is already in progress. The new Aeon has broken in with the Resurrection of Christ. Those believers bound up with Christ are no longer threatened by death. Even if they still die, they will be present at his near return by virtue of their connection with the Resurrected Lord, and will participate in his rule together with those who survive in a new corporeality. At the end of this period of messianic rule death will be completely overcome. Then the general resurrection of

the dead and the Last Judgment will occur. Then God
will be all in all (I Thess. 4:13ff., I Cor. 15, Rev. 20f.).

The doctrine of the Church which deals with Last
Things has moved these end-events into the distant future.
Already in the Second Epistle of Peter the original expectation of an imminent event is interpreted in such a way
that with the Lord a thousand years are as one day (2 Pet.
3:8). The Church has appeared in place of the messianic
time of the Lord—a fact which leads to the problem of
Chiliasm, the question of the beginning of the Thousand
Year Reign. Through its means of salvation the Church
grants to the believers immortality in the world beyond.
As a phenomenon spanning this world and the world beyond it fills out the long course of time before the end not
anticipated in the New Testament, and bestows upon it
the character of a supernatural *Heilsgeschichte*. In this
world this *Heilsgeschichte* consists in the preservation of
the Church and in the influences of the Church upon the
lives of individual believers to prepare them for the world
beyond. In the world beyond, according to Catholic dogma, the history of the souls continues in Hell, Purgatory
and Heaven, until someday at the end of time Christ will
return and with the Last Judgment will bring in the final
consummation.

This Catholic transformation of the primitive Christian
eschatology into a concept of *Heilsgeschichte* encompassing
this world and the next, time and eternity, was greatly
shaken when the Reformation with its concept of grace
broke the doctrine of Purgatory away from the system. In
this way a break was effected in *Heilsgeschichte* into which
at once quite different conceptions could flow, all of which
completely dispersed this formulation. In Neo-Protestantism there appeared in its place the ideas of a natural immortality of the soul and of an immanent development of

history, in which the Church ultimately had to play the role only of a cultural factor. In this modern faith in culture something of the dynamic of the primitive Christian expectation of the Kingdom of God was expressed over against the predominantly static character of the *Heilsgeschichte* of the Church. But this modern faith in the future of cultural development represented something quite different from the New Testament eschatology, and its idealistic faith in immortality was nourished from quite other sources than the primitive Christian mythology.

Nevertheless, the connection and inner necessity of the concepts of *Heilsgeschichte* and the world beyond with this history of these concepts should not be overlooked. After it became obvious that the eschatological mythology of primitive Christianity objectively understood and the reality of the actual course of history conceptually and objectively knowable came into open conflict, then the constant progressive transformation of this mythology was inevitable. That it led over and over to such transformations and that the message of the actuality of Last Things in the course of the catastrophes which it encountered was not simply discontinued—the reason for this is to be sought in the fact that in these different types of eschatology not merely the objectivity of mythology and speculative constructions was being dealt with, but rather self-understanding of existence was expressed in them and appeal was made to self-understanding and actualization of existence in space and time. To be sure, with the alternative of the objective forms of expression the self-understanding of existence expressed in them also changed. In the primitive Church, as well as in the Catholic and the Old and Neo-Protestant eschatology we are dealing not only with a mythology different in each case, but also in each with a different self-understanding of existence.

It cannot be the object of a theology which proceeds as the theology of existence from just this self-understanding of existence to exhaust itself in the criticism and defense of this or that eschatological concept with respect to its objectivity; rather, its task consists in initiating consideration and decision with respect to whether and to what extent we can know ourselves addressed by our eschatological heritage in our understanding of existence, and whether and to what extent the heritage can be useful to it as an appropriate expression. Corresponding to differences between individual and universal eschatology in the traditional doctrine of Last Things, the following is to be said:

Human life like all life is finite, transitory. We know no eternal, immortal life. All life dies, and we possess no experience that this process reverses itself, that an individual life lives again, that one who has died can be resuscitated. Nevertheless, there are such conceptions as immortality of the soul, life in another world, resurrection to eternal life. Christianity partially has these concepts in common with other religions or speculative philosophies; partly they are peculiar only to it, bound up with its concept of *Heilsgeschichte*, that is, with faith in the resurrection of Jesus and his return.

Scientifically such statements are all unprovable and untenable. They transcend the limits of what is scientifically verifiable and belong to the sphere of mythology and speculation. Precisely for this reason they are meaningful for existence. Immortality of the soul, concepts of the world beyond and belief in the resurrection are speculative-mythological forms of expression of the self-understanding of existence. In them existence brings to expression the claim that in view of its existence in time it is something quite other than what is comprehensible in the categories of space and time. Objectively regarded, the consciousness of existence is certainly bound up indissolubly with life in a mortal body. Taken objectively, all those statements about immortality and the world beyond are fantasies; they are products of the will, ideas born of fear of death, desires of the soul, exaggerations of the spirit, superstitions. But for existence which is conscious in the clarity of critical thinking of all these possible deviations, these speculative-mythological statements remain powerful as an expression of its faith. For existence, faith—certainly objectively not verifiable—is something quite different from an illusory product of vitality or of idealism; it is rather the becoming aware of its relation to Transcendence in the acceptance of its finitude as grace. As it is able to become aware of this faith out of those objectively misunderstood doctrines of a life after death, so it dares also to express its faith in these forms. The criterion of their truth and usefulness lies for existence only in the consideration that they can serve as an expression of its self-understanding in the tradition in which it finds itself.

Also dependent upon this consideration is what can be said in the context of a theology of existence in particular about life in the world beyond. The images used in this respect in the Christian tradition betray so much their earthly heritage in their particulars, from Purgatory and soul-sleep to the concepts of judgment, reunion and bliss, that a use of these for critical thinking other than a symbolic one, without which there is no genuine faith, is excluded at the outset. Why should not this whole image world of the region beyond, which forms the deposit of the existential understanding of centuries, be used and understood today by existence as a plastic expression of that which it, remaining in the world, experiences as guilt and redemption, illumination and unconditionality, fidelity and truth? In their mythological objectivity all of these concepts are bracketed as statements of truth by conceptual thinking—but the faith of existence supplies these brackets with a positive sign. The faith of existence here—corresponding to its own mythological forms of expression—deals with realities.

As in the traditional doctrine of Last Things universal eschatology first brings the fulfilment of individuals, so a corresponding interpretation of *Heilsgeschichte* belongs to the understanding of the concepts of the world beyond, as an expression of the self-understanding of existence, and is necessary for its completeness. Without the aspect of *Heilsgeschichte* the faith of existence also sinks only too easily into private interest in bliss. In the concepts of the world beyond there is certainly expressed the aspect of corporate involvement with others; but only the revelation of Christ for all the world, his victory over the powers, the general resurrection of the dead, the Last Judgment and the New Heaven and New Earth represent symbols for the communal context of existence as it shall be realized in the Church as Christian existence in community. Universal eschatology is the mythological expression of the nature of the Church as a phenomenon which appears and becomes operative in history. Christian existence in community reaches beyond the personal sphere and is of world-historical significance. This supra-individual character of existence is expressed in the mythology of the universal *Heilsgeschichte*.

Understood as mythology, the descriptions of the end-events do not speak of end-events which occur sometime in the course of time, or perhaps even in a distant future; rather they are nothing but the pictorially symbolic expression of the meaning and importance of the actualization of that reality which we have designated as Christian existence in community. In the dramatic event which encompasses the whole world, universal eschatology represents an illustration of the hope which the primitive Christian community attributed to Jesus: "Where two or three are gathered together in my name, there am I in the midst of them" (Matthew 18:20). Where existence understands and realizes itself in community, there occurs that which is meant in these mythological events. As they arose out of the self-understanding of existence in community, so their descriptions summon again to existence in community. In the use of the Word and the sacraments as means of salvation, salvation is present for existence in community, as it was expected in the Parousia, and the victorious struggle with the powers of the world begins, as it was described for the messianic reign. As described in the concept of the general resurrection of the dead, so here existence knows of its Transcendence in a responsibility which knows no limits. Here is enacted upon us the judgment upon our deeds; here it is a question of a final lostness and an eternal bliss which can only be received as grace. Here is enacted for the believer a transformation of his world, a new creation in which God is All in All. Christian existence in time is indeed eschatological existence.

Objectively, for this eschatology the world, time and history are not overcome. To the contrary: for existence the whole mythology is precisely an expression of its temporal disposition. The actualization of eschatology in its universal aspect stands, to be sure, in greatest opposition to its use as an objective scheme of a so-called *Heilsgeschichte*. The *Heilsgeschichte* of existence does not afford the opportunity of fixing the historical point of time at which humanity finds itself today between the Ascension and the Return of Jesus.

Nevertheless, for the understanding of the *Heilsgeschichte* from the perspective of existence significance is attached to the understanding of history, its meaning and the meaning of our existence in history. But it is not true that from the perspective of a *Heilsgeschichte*-mythology the meaning of history as a whole could be reconstructed, and from this reconstruction of total meaning the meaning of our existence in history could be determined. Such an understanding would be futile, both in view of the historically problematic character of the primitive Christian eschatology, and in respect to the limits of scientific knowledge which permit no total perspective. That history as a whole has a meaning and a goal is rather a mythology or speculation in which only the faith of existence can express symbolically its self-understanding. So understood, these symbols do not allow themselves to be used in a theoretical perspective, but possess their truth only in the realization of existence which is understood in each of the historical situations. Existence knows no other meaning of history than that which is given to it in its realization in community. Apart from this community and the tradition out of which it arises and which it continues through its self-realization, it possesses no experience. To the extent, however, that grace is given to it to realize itself in community, it sees itself in its history placed in a *Heilsgeschichte*. About these realizations of salvation as manifestations of the infinite creative possibilities of God—realizations which are connected, but not to be systematized beforehand—the theology of existence avows: "Of his fulness we have all received, grace unto grace" (John 1:16). In this—its true *Heilsgeschichte*—it rests content.